GLOUCESTER MASSACHUSETTS

ROCKPORT PUBLISHERS

The Perfectly
Painted House

A FOOLPROOF GUIDE FOR CHOOSING EXTERIOR PAINT COLORS

Bonnie Rosser Krims

First published in the United States of America by
Rockport Publishers, Inc.
33 Commercial Street
Gloucester, Massachusetts 01930-5089
Telephone: (978) 282-9590
Facsimile: (978) 283-2742
www.rockpub.com

ISBN 1-56496-853-7

10 9 8 7 6 5 4 3 2 1

Design: Casey Design, Worcester, Massachusetts
Cover Images: Brian Vanden Brink, left, middle;
Eric Roth, right

Printed in China.

Be aware that some paint colors may have been changed by the publisher without color testing by the author. The author bears no responsibility for any such changes regarding paint brands and colors.

Grateful acknowledgment is given to the following for permission to use their paint color numbers, though the four-color process colors used in printing this book may not exactly match each manufacturer's paint chip colors: Benjamin Moore and Co., Sherwin-Williams Paints (The Sherwin-Williams Co.), Pittsburgh Paints (PPG Architectural Finishes, Inc.), PPG Industries, Inc., California Paints and California Paints' Historic Colors of America (California Products Corp.)

Paint manufacturers routinely reevaluate their color systems. Consequently, you may encounter a few colors for which sample paint chips are unavailable. However, paint in these colors will still be available. Simply use the discontinued color numbers to obtain the paint from your paint store.

Contents

Introduction

Since the publication of my book on interior wall paint color, people have been asking when I will write a book on exterior paint colors.

Choosing exterior colors is a much more daunting task, involving far more financial and aesthetic risk than choosing interior colors. The task baffles many people. To date, no reliable resources were available for guidance.

Paint color is the single most effective way to change the personality of your house and transform it to its best advantage. Paint color can change the appearance of your home's size, making it seem larger or smaller, taller or wider. It can highlight aspects of the architecture. Paint can make your house stand out from or blend into its surroundings, whichever you desire. To an undistinguished home, properly chosen paint color can add a new sense of design and style.

Color selection is not easy. Paint chips are small and houses are large. The simplest solution would be to find a house similar in style to your own that is painted in colors you love and ask the occupants what colors they used. If only it were that easy! Many of you don't know what color you want your house to be. Others know you want yellow, for instance, but don't know which specific yellow to choose from the thousands available.

Many who want to do what will be considered in good taste are puzzled to know what colors to use, and how to direct their painter so as to give him a tolerably clear idea of what they want. —Ehrick Kensett Rossiter and Frank Ayers Wright, *Modern House Painting,* 1882

You don't want to make a paint color mistake on your house. It's far too costly. Using this book, you can rest assured you will choose the right colors. I show you everything you need to know, including optimum color coordination of the house, the trim, shutters, window boxes, and so on. Consideration is also given to flowers, shrubs, and walkways. You will have the exact paint color numbers in hand when you are ready to purchase paint. In addition, you will have all the information you need to ensure a lasting paint job. After all, you are protecting and preserving your largest investment from the elements. I answer your color questions—"What color should I paint the garage door?"—and technical questions—"What kind of surface preparation does my stucco home need before painting?" "How much should it cost to have my house painted?"

The Perfectly Painted House *comprises three sections. The first covers introductory material on choosing house paint colors, including step-by-step guidelines and information on the painting process itself. The main body of the text offers color recipes—ready-made color combinations for the exterior of the house.*

This section is subdivided by color: red, orange, yellow, green, blue, violet, and the neutral colors (white, gray, and brown). Each color section presents five or more recipes that provide variations on a single color. For example, the yellow section includes five photographs of yellow houses, each displaying a different yellow. I isolated some of the best exterior yellow paint colors from a wide range of reputable paint manufacturers, saving you the trouble of weeding through hundreds of yellow paint chips.

Most readers will find pictured a style of house similar to their own to use as a launching point for selecting color. As you leaf through the recipes, identify photographs of homes like yours. This will help guide you with color selection, as some colors are more appropriate to certain styles than others. The exterior features on the houses in these photographs may not match yours, but if your house shares certain characteristics, such as a similar house style, you may want to consider that color recipe. For example, the exterior details of your Victorian may not match those of the Victorians in this book—yours may be simpler or more elaborate. Don't let this stop you from taking your color cues from the recipes provided.

Throughout the text, you'll find inspirational narrative and quotations that describe the mood or character each color evokes. These are meant to convey more about the style of each house and excite you about the possibility of painting.

Specific paint manufacturer color numbers are included with each recipe. Additional color options are provided for use on decorative elements (doors, shutters, window boxes, window trim, etc.). Some colors create an austere or formal look while others are playful. Although the photograph in a recipe may show a yellow house with a black door, you can, of course, decide on other door or shutter colors that suit you and the look you wish to create.

The third section of the book consists of two appendices. Appendix A (page 130) is about creating color schemes. Appendix B (page 134) is about American architecture with respect to exterior paint color.

Until now, choosing exterior paint colors meant going to the paint store, looking through paint chips or brochures, and exercising a great leap of faith. I made your task easier by sifting through the colors, carefully selecting and combining them, and showing you how they look on a house. The Perfectly Painted House *helps you make color choices while avoiding most of the difficulty associated with the job. This book also serves as a practical guide to the logistics of painting a house. Finally, you won't find the exterior colors in this book wildly dramatic or shockingly vivid. This is a practical guide for real people living in real homes, not a coffee-table book of unusual exteriors and show homes. All of these features make* The Perfectly Painted House *both unique and useful.*

Getting Started

Tuning In to House Color

All styles of architecture have had definable color palettes. Greek Revival and late Federal houses were predominantly white. Pale earth tones dominated early Victorian homes. Dark, rich colors ruled during the high Victorian phase and, eventually, the Colonial Revival saw a return to white and light pastels.

For our purposes, however, choosing a color scheme involves only identifying colors you like and combining them appropriately with the fixed colors surrounding your house (walkways, stone walls, roof, fences) and the nearby landscaping.

Start by looking at other houses for inspiration. Search out homes that match the architectural style of your house.

You can learn a lot from their color successes and misses. Take pictures of them. Collect photos from magazines, too, as well as exterior paint color brochures from your local paint store. Determine your color preferences. What colors attract you? Consider features of your home that may limit your paint color choices. For example, its fixed colors (brick front, stone front, terra-cotta roof, stained natural or painted wood, deck, patio, pathway, foundation) are already part of its color scheme. If these features won't be painted, they must be factored in. However, the more neutral the fixed colors are (gray shingled roof, blacktop driveway, cement foundation), the less weight they will carry in your decision. If your home is historic, your town may restrict paint color choices.

I understand how scarlet can differ from crimson because I know that the smell of an orange is not the smell of a grapefruit. —Helen Keller

The recipes in this book offer a personal, easy, quick, and reliable approach to choosing paint colors. If you wish to do more research, look at paint color manufacturers' chips and strips. Each strip shows five to ten relative values of a color, and each manufacturer offers 1200 to 2000 colors. But not many people can visualize colors on a house using paint chips. If you go this route, compare your favorite chip colors to the colors in this book. This will help you gauge whether or not the colors are appropriate or too light, too dark, or too intense for your home. For a technical approach, see Appendix A, which describes using the color wheel to make color selections.

Fixed Features

Now that you have considered the colors of other homes, let's focus on your house, its fixed features, and its surroundings.

Let's also consider the atmosphere you wish to create. Your repainted house is a revealing public presentation of you, so it is important to spend time evaluating your house (see the following lists) before making decisions. Take the time to observe and evaluate all of the fixed features of your house. Write down any point that is applicable to you.

Stand outside and look at your house as a whole. Imagine it all white. This will help you focus on the details. How intricate are the door and window frames? Should they be emphasized? Are the windows arranged symmetrically or asymmetrically? Notice the sashes (on a double-hung window, the portions of the window that move up and down) and the number of doors and their place-

ment. Notice the roofline. Are the eaves (the projecting lower edge or edges of a roof) open or boxed? Note the patterns of brick, stone, or wood, if present on your house. Observe the location and vertical lines of the downspouts. Which lines or forms on your house, if any, would you consider emphasizing with color? Which would you rather fade into the background?

Jot down any detail that strikes you as pertinent to paint color selection. You might think the trim would look great painted in a contrasting color. Perhaps your window sashes could be painted to contrast with the trim. Evaluate their width. Are they wide enough to accent with a color? Focus your attention on the landscape colors. What colors predominate? Do you think they should affect your house paint color choices? Do you plan new landscaping?

How to Assess Fixed Features

Roof

If your roof is neutral—gray or black, for instance—you can make your color plan without regard to its color. If it is more colorful, you must include it in your overall color scheme. Identify the color of your roof. If you live in an older house, it is probably one of the following:

- slate—purple, gray-black, blue-black, purple-red, or green
- wooden shingle—brown or gray
- metal—unpainted copper, usually dark red, dark reddish-brown, or dark olive
- ceramic tile—terra-cotta, yellow, yellow to brownish-red, red, green, or blue

Newer houses usually feature composition roofing of asphalt or fiberglass in any of these colors.

Masonry

Does your home feature significant brick and stonework on the house, pathways, patios, or garden walls? Unpainted concrete is neutral, but brick and stone have plenty of color. If colored masonry is prominent, you must factor it into your color scheme. Alternatively, you can paint it as part of a new color scheme.

Downspouts and Gutters

Downspouts and gutters should almost always be inconspicuously painted. If the house trim is white, they should probably be white too. If they are copper, allow them to oxidize naturally.

Awnings

Awnings are usually made of canvas and have a color and a pattern. If their color is neutral, chances are you needn't consider them. If they are striped in blue and white, they must be factored into your color scheme.

Plants

Trees, grass, flowers, and ornamental plantings are considered fixed features. With respect to your color scheme, focus on their spring and summer colors. Bright fall foliage is fleeting, and the browns and grays of winter are neutral and, therefore, have limited effect on the color scheme.

Nature combines colors in ways that we don't dare, so choose landscape–house color combinations that please you. If a magenta rhododendron is planted close to a brown house and the colors seem out of sync, either move the plant or add more of the same to accentuate the color. There is color strength in numbers, but you must like the color combination.

Continued on next page

Other Buildings

If a shed, separated garage, barn, or doghouse is visible with your house, its materials, if they are colored, must be factored in or painted to coordinate with the main building.

Wood and Metal

Stained, varnished, or painted wood, as well as metal, should be factored into your scheme. Fences, gates, and decks, especially right next to the house, must be treated as fixed features or repainted.

Wood and metal both have color. Oak is a light- to medium-value brown; mahogany is a darker, warmer brown, and cherry is a lighter, redder brown. Though they are all basically brown, they shift toward other hues—yellow, pink, red, green, blue, etc. Iron and steel, galvanized metal, aluminum, copper, and brass also have color. If these materials are going to remain unpainted, you must treat them as fixed features when choosing paint colors.

Foundation

On most homes, the foundation is neutral in color. If yours is stone or brick and looks attractive, don't paint it. The foundation of Victorian homes was often painted a dark brick red. Their original owners didn't plant in front of them to avoid harboring insects.

Water Table

The board below the siding of clapboard buildings is called the water table. Customarily, it is painted to match the trim color.

Steps

On wooden steps, the treads (the steps themselves) usually carry the porch or deck color while the risers (the vertical pieces between the steps) are normally painted the house trim color.

Porch

Porches were traditionally painted with gray floors and blue ceilings; the reflected light was practical, and the blue suggested the sky. The gray floors also showed little dust and tracking. But porch floors can be painted any color. A good choice is the color of the housebody or trim, if not too dark or too light. Ceilings can be stained, varnished, or painted the housebody color. The trim color is a good choice for the rafters. Wooden porch posts are usually painted in the trim color. If you like, paint a decorative floor (remembering its high maintenance when it comes to repainting). Paint alternate floorboards in two colors to create stripes, or do a neoclassical checkerboard in light and dark blocks.

Balustrades	Balustrades are two parallel rails, held in place by porch posts or pedestals, with the space between them occupied by a row of balusters. They enclose balconies, staircases, terraces, and so on. The balustrades are sometimes painted darker than the rails.
Porch Grill or Latticework	The grill or latticework under the porch can be painted with consideration to its size. If it is large (5–6 feet or 1.5–1.6 meters), a dark color will camouflage it. If it is short (1–3 feet or .3–.9 meters), paint it the house body color, trim color, or white.

Windows

In the nineteenth century, window sashes and frames were usually painted the same color. Sometimes the sashes were painted darker. After 1876, sashes and frames were differentiated; the sash was painted darker, except on white Colonial Revival houses. The storm windows are always the same color as the sash.

Evaluate your windows. If they have elaborate trim (Victorian houses do), you may decide to highlight it by using a darker color on the receding or sunken parts (called shadows). If the housebody is light, painting the facings of the windows, the cornices, and so on, in a darker shade of the same color will make them seem to project outward. You could reverse this scenario by painting a lighter color on the receding or sunken parts and painting the facings of the windows in a lighter tint of the house color. If your house has detailed trim, refer to a good book on Victorian houses for accurate color selection and application.

If your windows have white vinyl trim that cannot be painted, you should probably have white house trim too.

Shutters

In the nineteenth century, shutters were essential for protection and were almost always painted dark green. Later, lighter tints or darker shades of the house color were used, with a preference for darker colors. Sometimes shutters are painted using the trim color. This is a good place to be creative.

Doors

Assess materials first: steel, wood, fiberglass, screen door, storm door. You can paint almost any material if you use the correct type of paint. Paint screen and storm doors the same color as the main door, or use the trim color. With main doors, your options are varied. You can stain and varnish them to display the natural wood grain. If your wood door isn't naturally beautiful wood, you can paint it using faux-finish graining to simulate wood. You can paint it in a contrasting color that complements the color of the house, or use the trim color. Door frames can be painted the same color as the house or the trim color. You might use a darker shade of the trim color for sunken panels on the door and a medium shade for the stiles (the vertical struts on paneled doors).

Choosing Colors

Now that you have made some important determinations about your house's fixed features and its surroundings, let us focus on methods for choosing color.

We will use the recipes in this book and their accompanying photographs. This approach is creative and enjoyable. You can also refer to Appendix A if you are interested in the color wheel approach to color scheme creation.

As you go through the recipe sections, consider how the house color, trim color, and decorative detail colors affect the mood you want your house to set in addition to whether the colors contrast or blend in with the surroundings.

Trim and detail colors always affect the character a house conveys. The colors of brick and stone can be formal and austere or familiar and gracious, depending on the paint colors used on the accompanying trim and decorative details. Imagine a brick-fronted Federal house with black shutters. Picture the same house with pale blue shutters. This change makes a difference in the overall mood the house creates. Pale blue seems friendlier than reserved black. Imagine the difference between a white clapboard house with dark green shutters and doors and the same white house with red shutters and doors. Green is the traditional shutter color choice. It is staid, blending in with its surroundings, the trees and grass. Red, being the complement of green, stands out from its surroundings. It is a more dynamic, livelier choice than green.

Four Steps for Choosing Exterior Paint Color

Step 1

General Color

Choose one or two color sections from this book to focus on based on your personal color preferences. I chose the yellow and white sections because my house is in the Colonial style and for years I have admired traditional white and yellow Colonials. I wanted a color to reflect light and look bright. Also, I felt that the colors of my landscape (lots of pink, white, blue, and red blossoms) and my fixed fixtures (a red brick walk) would stand out against a white or yellow backdrop.

Now stand outside and imagine one of the colors you selected on your house. In my case, that was white. How will it look with your fixed features, the colors of your shrubs, flowers, and so on? How will it look on your specific lot? Will it make the house stand out or blend in? How will the color look next to the homes abutting it (if they are close to

your house)? Will the color work on the style of your home? Evaluate this color. Once you are satisfied that you have fully imagined it on the house, go through the same exercise using your second possible color.

Step 2

Specific Color

Narrow your choice to just one color section using step 1. In my case, I realized that a big white house would be a little too prominent on our small corner lot. The house was formerly a pale beige-brown. White was too striking a contrast. Yellow, on the other hand, was still bright and pleasant but would not overpower the house or the lot. Yellow added interest and color but was less a contrast with the landscape than white. Make these determinations for your house, and narrow your focus to just one color section.

Step 3

Reassess

Now that you know the color you will be evaluating on your house (in my case, yellow), look over all the recipes in that color section. You will see five or more houses, each painted in a variation of that color. Choose one or two of your favorite recipes from the section. Let the style of your house and the style of the houses pictured help you. Write down the paint color numbers of your favorite(s). You will test the colors you choose before painting the entire house. Often, the final colors are determined using a process of elimination at the testing stage. Pick what you think is your best choice, and take your color cues for the door and additional decorative elements from suggestions in the recipe and other houses you have observed. Don't finalize any of your trim or accompanying colors until you test your main color.

Step 4

Testing the Paint Color(s)

View the colors all together on your house. For each color you are testing, buy a quart of paint, a stir stick, and a disposable foam brush. You should also purchase a drop cloth or lay down newspaper to catch drips and spills. Sample each color directly on the house. You don't need to paint a large area—just enough to determine if you like the colors, about 2 feet by 2 feet (.6 m by .6 m). If you like a color, test it again over a larger area—about 5 feet by 5 feet (1.5 m by 1.5 m). Test the colors on doors and trim also. You don't need to paint the whole door. Paint just enough of it to determine whether the color suits you and whether the color works well with the housebody color. I cannot emphasize the importance of testing colors directly on the house enough. This is the only way to assess how they will actually look. Testing colors on a board or posterboard is inadequate. Believe me, I am speaking from experience.

Colors look different on a house than on chips. In addition, the same color paint will look different on clapboard than it does on wooden shingles. It will look different in the sun than it does in the shade (because light affects color), so apply tests in sunny and shady areas. View these test patches at different times of the day. Apply at least two coats of paint for your test patches. Wait for paint to dry completely before making a decision. Latex reaches its true color in one hour, alkyd (oil) in 24 hours.

If you are basically satisfied with a color but want to make subtle adjustments, don't hesitate to ask for help. Paint dealers can lighten, darken, or temper your colors. This testing and adjusting is worth your time and effort. Don't let impatience get the better of you. Make sure you are satisfied before investing in paint, labor, and money.

Once your paint dealer makes the color adjustments (if any), test your colors on the house again until they meet your satisfaction. Now you are ready to paint the house. If you find that the color simply doesn't work the way you had hoped, move on. Choose another color to evaluate and repeat these steps.

Keep in mind that the photographs on these pages have undergone a printing process that alters their actual color. Therefore, while you can use these photos as a guide to determine your color preferences, rely on the actual paint chip color numbers, the corresponding chips found at your paint dealership, and your color test to make your final decisions.

Painting the House

Hiring a Painter

If you are hiring a painter, get two or three estimates. Ask friends and neighbors, as well as your local paint store, for referrals.

You want someone who can do a great job at a price you can afford and with whom you are comfortable working. Ask the paint contractors the following questions before they visit your house:

1. Are you licensed? Make sure the painter you hire is licensed. This gives you some protection if you are not happy with the work. Each state has its own standards of performance for paint contractors and has different means of addressing customer grievances.

2. Do you have insurance? Your painter should carry liability insurance. In the event that your property is damaged, you will have the security that the contractor is responsible for fixing it.

3. Do you guarantee your work? Your painter should guarantee his work. Paint manufacturers guarantee their paint up to twenty years. Weather, quality of materials, and excellent prep determine how long the paint will last.

4. Who will do the work? Some companies bid out paint jobs to other contractors. You want to know who is actually doing the work and be sure that the supervisor on the job understands the job. You also must ensure that the subcontract is exactly the same as the original contract to which you agreed. You need to be comfortable working with the supervisor.

5. What is your preferred brand of paint? Many painters use one brand of paint exclusively. If you have a different preference, ask the painter if he is willing use it. Often, painters will offer to match paint colors in your preferred brand using their brand. A perfect match is impossible, and even subtle color changes make a huge difference on an area as large as a house, so beware.

Once you receive the estimates and decide on a painter, arrange a written schedule for the work and the payment. Don't assume that your painters will start and finish your job before moving on to the next. Many painters juggle multiple jobs at once. They may show up at your house on day one and not again for two weeks. Painting does depend on the weather, so make allowances for rain.

Be sure to agree to, and list in writing, any special requests that you have, such as daily starting and quitting times, whether you permit use of a radio, disposing of paint, cleanup requirements, even whether dogs or kids are allowed on the job (you'd be surprised).

Calculating the Size of Your House

The best way to assess a contractor's estimate

is to approximate one yourself. Whether you do your own work or not, you should estimate the amount of time and materials needed. Use these simple guidelines:

Step 1

Calculate the size of the house.

1. Measure the width of the house.	Run a tape measure along the base.
2. Measure the height of the house.	To measure the height of a two-story house, pick a point about half way up, measure to that point, then double the result.
3. Calculate the square footage of the house.	You don't need to make deductions for doors, as there are only a few. Use common sense to deduct footage for windows. Make adjustments for large surfaces on the house not to be painted.

Step 2

Estimate time.

Aside from the actual painting, you need to include time for daily setup, cleanup, breaks, meals, runs to store for materials, and weather interruptions.

Housebody	for a painter to roll and brush smooth siding (e.g., clapboard) on a house:	100–150 square feet (30.5–45.7 m)/hour
	for a painter to roll and brush a medium-textured stucco wall:	200 square feet (61 m)/hour
	for a painter to roll and brush shingles:	80–125 square feet (24.4–38.1 m)/hour
Windows *calculated by the number of panes, or lights, of glass*	ordinary sash window: (1 light over 1 light):	20 minutes
	ordinary sash window: (6 lights over 1 light):	40 minutes
	ordinary sash window: (12 lights):	60 minutes
Doors *standard sizes*	plain:	15 minutes
	paneled:	45 minutes
	louvered:	45 minutes
Miscellaneous	louvered shutters, 2 feet by 4 feet (.6 m by 1.2 m) (both sides):	45 minutes
	simple wrought-iron railing:	20 linear feet (6.1 m)/hour
	decorated wrought-iron railing:	10 linear feet (3 m)/hour
	simple wooden railing:	15 linear feet (4.6 m)/hour
	wide eaves:	50 square feet (15.2 m)/hour

Step 3

Estimate materials.

Paint coverage depends on the porosity of the surface it is deposited on. Obviously, unpainted plaster is more porous than primed wood. The following figures are for a surface of average porosity.

Acrylic (latex) paint (square yards/square meter)	
primer/undercoat:	55 (46 sq. m)
paint finish coat:	82 (69 sq. m)
masonry paint (smooth surface):	65 (54 sq. m)
masonry paint (rough surface):	22 (18 sq. m)
wood stain:	110 (92 sq. m)

Oil-based (alkyd) paint (square yards/square meter)	
primer:	110 (92 sq. m)
undercoat:	82 (69 sq. m)
paint finish coat:	92 (76 sq. m)
oil:	65 (54 sq. m)
wood preservative:	55 (46 sq. m)
varnish:	87 (73 sq. m)
wood stain:	120 (100 sq. m)

Choosing
Paint and Stain

Whether you choose to paint or stain, buy high-quality materials. Low-cost paint that yields poor coverage can end in disaster.

It's better to start with good materials. You will need to determine the sheen best suited for each of the surfaces to be painted (high gloss, semigloss, flat, etc.). Every paint brand has its own terms for these sheens. Gloss or sheen is the degree to which a painted surface reflects light. High gloss, semigloss, satin finish, eggshell, low luster, and matte (or flat) finish are typical names for a manufacturer's glosses.

- High gloss looks wet and shiny.
- Semigloss is shiny and smooth but not wet looking. It is the most common sheen used for trim.
- Eggshell, satin, and low luster fall in the middle between flat and high gloss.
- Matte or flat finish looks like unglazed tile or chalk.

Choosing the level of gloss is an aesthetic decision. Be aware, however, that high gloss shows imperfections more than any other sheen and, therefore, requires more careful preparation. Time and weather reduce the gloss level.

You must further choose among the following three types of paint:

1. oil-based paint, in which the vehicle or binder is a drying oil, such as linlinseed or soy
2. latex paint, in which the vehicle is a water-based emulsion
3. solvent products, including varnishes and specialty finishes

All paint products go from a liquid state through various stages of drying to a full cure. Many oil-based paints must be dry for six, eight, or up to twenty-four hours before recoating. Latex requires between one and three hours.

Paint and Stain Options

Latex	The main advantages of latex are low odor, easy cleanup, short drying time, superior build, and low sensitivity to alkali in the surface, which is important when painting over cement or plaster.
Oil	Although oil-based paints take longer to dry, they dry harder than latex, hold much better, are impermeable, and are more resistant to abrasion.
Alkyd-modified latex	These latex house paints contain modified alkyd resins and offer the best of both worlds—latex and oil.
Stain	Stains contain the same basic ingredients as paint and are applied in the same way. They are also available in latex and oil-based versions. Whereas paint is solid and opaque, stain penetrates the surface to reveal the natural color and texture of wood. Natural stains make the least change in the color of the wood because they have the least pigment. When using stain, there is no need to smooth or prime the surface wood. Stain doesn't last as long as paint because it has less build.
Semitransparent stain	These stains have more pigment than natural stains but still allow some natural color to show through.
Opaque stain	These stains have enough pigment to make solid colors but allow more natural texture of the surface to show than paint does. They also produce the lowest sheen available.
Penetrating color sealer	Clear or tinted, these stains correspond to transparent interior wood stains for use on new or unfinished wood or wood previously treated with the same product.
Porch and deck paint	Surfaces subject to extra-heavy wear (including thresholds) should be painted with a product specifically formulated to resist abrasion and foot traffic. These paints are available in latex and oil-based formulations.

(Note: Redwood and cedar contain water-soluble substances that can stain through latex paints. They must be sealed with an oil-based product before they can be painted with latex.)

Preparation before Painting

Proper surface preparation is the most critical part of the paint job.

If your house is in good shape and you are only changing the color, preparation should take only one-half or one-quarter of the time it takes to apply one coat of paint to the house. If, however, there is peeling paint or deterioration, the prep time will be longer—about the same time as it takes to apply one coat of paint. If paint is peeling over a small part of the house, remove the loose paint, spot prime, and apply the finish coat. This approach may take as long as applying one full coat of paint to the house. If you want to make the house look like new, scrape and prime the entire house. Applying this coat of primer would not count as prep time because you are actually painting the entire house with it. It would be calculated as paint time.

If you have good prep work, the new paint will adhere to the building for five years or more. If you have poor prep, the paint job will last only about two years. Basic prep includes these tasks:

- Protect plants, window glass, and other unpainted surfaces.
- Power wash the house.
- Kill mildew.
- Remove loose paint, spot prime bare wood, and spot prime metal on the same day (to prevent rusting).
- Smooth surface by sanding or stripping old paint.
- Repair loose or missing glazing from windows before priming.
- Etch, clean, and prime bare galvanized steel with metal primer.
- Patch holes and cracks in wood, stucco, and metal, then sand patches smooth.
- Caulk.
- Apply full coat of primer if necessary.

Primers

The primer provides a surface for paint to adhere to. It also protects and seals the surface. You can tint the primer using your base color for better paint color coverage. Tint the primer slightly lighter than the base coat color (so as not to confuse them). Once you have primed the house, you must paint soon after (within weeks is best), as primer should not be exposed to weather for long. Some primers can be applied and finish coated the same day. Many need twenty-four hours to cure. Discuss the type of primer to use with your paint dealer.

(Note: Each metal surface has its own preparation requirements. Talk with your paint dealer.)

Masonry Prep

Most masonry finishes have a life expectancy of up to ten years. However, without good surface preparation, that may be cut in half. Masonry prep involves these tasks:

- Scrape loose materials, such as paint and lichen.
- Check for mold and algae and apply fungicide (allow twenty-four hours for fungicide to kill mold), then wash with clean water.
- When walls are dry, rub your hand across them to check for chalky or powdery texture. Treat those areas with a stabilizing solution to bind the surface and make it ready to accept paint.
- Repair any surface flaw larger than a hairline crack with exterior filler or cement, depending on the severity of the cracks or holes.
- Prime with masonry primer.

Common Problems Requiring Prep

Chalking	Existing paint looks like it has a layer of chalk dust. Run your finger across it. If you pick up a layer of residue, you will need to wash the house with trisodium phosphate (TSP) or another strong detergent. Work from the top down with a scrub brush or use a power washer.
Mildew	Wash mildewed areas with chlorine bleach solution and soap. Use 3 parts soapy water to I part bleach.
Metal stains	Wash stains off wood before priming. Prime metal before painting to keep stain from bleeding onto wood.
Rot	Dry or wet rot must be removed or killed with a biocide. Patch holes. Stabilize damage with resinous wood hardener. Patch with resin fillers.
Knots	Spot prime knots with pigmented shellac (latex or oil-based) to seal out the resin.
Nail holes	Fill with exterior spackle compound or linseed oil putty.
Uneven, chipped, or peeling paint	Scrape (go with the grain) and sand or strip if necessary before priming using a heat gun or chemical stripper.
Cracks	Use exterior spackle compound to fill small cracks in wood siding, cracks or gaps between different kinds of building materials (e.g., wood and masonry, wood and metal, plastic and metal; also joints between two pieces of wood in a window or door frame), and small cracks in stucco. Repair large cracks in stucco with stucco patch. Repair large cracks in wood with resin fillers.
Cracked window glazing	If window glaze has shallow surface cracks, add new glazing compound over it. If glaze is badly cracked, use a heat gun to remove old compound back to a clean sash, prime, and reglaze the window.
Alligatoring and crazing	These paint conditions are caused by paint drying faster than it should or by putting on too thick a coat of paint. Scrape, sand, and patch affected areas before priming.

Blistering	This condition is caused by painting over surface dirt or moist wood. Moisture is trying to escape from behind the paint. Scrape and sand affected areas before priming.
Efflorescence	This condition, in which salts crystallize on a masonry surface, is caused by mineral salts reacting with water. Scrape away deposits and let dry completely. Use only water-based paints, which allow remaining water or moisture to dry through the painted surface.
Loose plaster	The plaster layer on a wall sometimes breaks away from its blockbase, making the wall surface unstable. Plaster tends to break down in localized areas. Loose plaster should always be removed and the surface patched.
Rust stains	This brownish staining is caused by external metal fixtures or old nails that corrode and wash down masonry walls in the rain. Paint all metal fixtures, then clean stained areas and seal them with an oil-based undercoat.

◼ Preparation Tips for Metal and Vinyl

Vinyl gutters	No primer needed. Use one or two coats of gloss paint.
Metal gutters	Use commercial metal paints for all except aluminum.
Metal windows	Use metal primer.
Aluminum and vinyl windows	Do not paint.
Galvanized metals	Use specially designed primer.
Metal garage doors	Use metal primer, undercoat, then one or two coats of gloss paint.

Painting

To be sure that your primer and paint will bond to the surface paint, paint in the right weather—mild and dry. Don't paint in direct sunlight. Start early in the day so paint can dry before the evening dew falls. The ideal conditions are 70°F (21°C) with little to no breeze.

Paint the house in this order:

1

Scrape old paint.

2

Prime scraped areas.

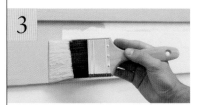

3

Paint eaves and overhangs.
Paint housebody.

4

Paint trim and dimensional details (windows, doors, railings, decks, thresholds, steps).

For all surfaces:

- Work from the top down and the inside out.
- Apply flat paints before gloss paints, as they are easier to touch up than gloss.
- Save areas to be stained for last.
- Reach a visual breakpoint before you stop painting, especially for gloss finishes.
- Paint doors and windows early in the day so they will dry before being closed and locked at night.
- Let one color dry before painting another next to it.

Apply all exterior finishes in the right order

Alkyd Paint on Bare Wood	1. bare wood 2. sealer on bare wood knots 3. primer or preservative primer 4. undercoat 5. paint
Latex Paint on Bare Wood	1. bare wood 2. sealer on bare wood knots 3. primer undercoat 4. paint
Masonry Paint on New Plaster	1. bare plaster 2. first coat masonry paint 3. second coat masonry paint
Masonry Paint on Old Plaster	1. old painted masonry surface 2. fungicide 3. stabilizing solution/primer 4. first coat masonry paint 5. second coat masonry paint

Wood Stain	1. bare wood
	2. preservative base coat
	   (solvent-based products only)
	3. first coat stain
	4. second coat stain
	   (third coat may be required
	   for water-based products)

Varnish	1. bare wood 2. preservative base coat 3. first coat varnish 4. second coat varnish

Metal Finishing Paint	1. bare or previously painted metal
	2. first coat proprietary metal
	   finishing paint
	3. second coat metal finishing paint
	   if necessary

Finally, be sure to keep some of the paint and finish that you use for touch-ups or to match colors later.

Red is the great clarifier—

bright, cleansing, and revealing. It makes all colors look beautiful.
I can't imagine getting bored with red—it would be like getting
bored with the person you love. —Diana Vreeland

Red houses look beautiful all year in their surroundings. During the winter, red houses are warm and lively against the white snow, beckoning us to enter. In summer, red houses are highlighted by fresh green lawns, draping foliage, and blossoming bushes. Red houses glow in the sunlight among the colors of fall foliage—crimson, gold, and amber.

From brick to ruby, there is a red for every architectural style. Whether you live in a Vermont-style farmhouse, a Gothic, Spanish, art deco, Victorian, or Dutch Colonial, red is a fabulous paint color choice. Reds range from hot crimson and scarlet to cherry, cranberry, and clay, and on into pink. It takes confidence to paint your house red, but lovers of red tend to be self-assured and secure individuals to begin with.

Care to lighten up? Pink is friendly, even playful, and tells your visitors that hospitality lies within. Some pinks are whimsical—tropic pinks and cotton candy. Other desirable pinks are elegant rose and friendly magenta. If your house is stucco, try a light rose with gray-green trim to evoke the Caribbean, the Greek isles, or Florida's South Beach. A dramatic statement can be made by painting a wood clapboard house raspberry with black shutters and white trim.

If you are not up to painting your whole house red, create a focal point by painting it on the front door. Berry red is a lovely welcome to guests and is recommended by practitioners of the ancient Chinese art of feng shui as a front door color because it invites prosperity. You can choose to paint the shutters red to create a cottage look. How about red deck paint on your porch? There are many places red can work its magic.

Use your imagination as you go through the recipes that follow. You'll love being "the neighbor in the red house!"

Raspberry Jewel Deep Violet Red

Simple things become beautiful and attractive by an art inspiration. Homes retain their old forms substantially, but they put on new faces when touched by the real artist.

—Palliser, *Palliser's American Architecture*, 1888

Sometimes the gray days of winter feel so long. Spring seems elusive. And then you see something beautiful that renews your spirit—COLOR! The color of raspberries. It is the dead of winter, yet this heartwarming red-raspberry house stands in vibrant contrast to the white snow, reminding us of the importance of well-chosen color.

The raspberry clapboard is perfectly complemented by the blue-green door and window sashes. The house attains a complete visual balance through its inherent symmetry and its carefully chosen color scheme. The cream-colored window frames, eaves, and door panels provide contrast and make the raspberry and blue-green house colors pop. Stenciled patterns on the door panels and a thick boxwood garland draped around the door add elegance to the otherwise simple facade of this Colonial house.

Fixed features include the granite steps, walk, and stone wall—all gray, with hints of blue. The blue door color picks up the tones of these elements. Landscaping in the front yard is primarily green shrubbery echoing the blue-green of the door, with white accents. In spring and summer, assorted flowers are displayed in decorative pots. This is a truly wonderful combination. No additional colors are necessary.

Housebody color:	1. Benjamin Moore—Old Claret 2083-30
Trim color:	2. Benjamin Moore—Monterey White HC-27
Details:	3. Benjamin Moore—Crystal Lake 353-4

For a Different Look

If this house color is too bright, daring, or edgy for your tastes, choose a less purple red. A redder red will still look beautiful, but will have a slightly more traditional appearance. Door and trim colors can remain the same.

Perfectly Painted:

To add charm to your home, add decorative painting to the front door, such as this stenciled door panel.

Enigmatic Pink

Rose Blush

The very pink of perfection. —Oliver Goldsmith

This old Victorian extravaganza looks perky in pink. It expresses both lightheartedness and a sense of solidity and sturdiness. Pink gives a whimsical lift but still exemplifies a rather sophisticated color choice. Why does the house seem to elicit such contradictory reactions? Because pink has a split personality. Pink consists of red and white, and each of these colors causes different reactions. Bluer pinks take on many of the serene qualities of blue. Likewise, redder pinks take on the dynamic qualities of red. Add gray to the mix, and the color becomes subdued and low-key. Pink conjures a wide variety of reactions in everyone who views it. How does it strike you? Isn't it a great way to enliven the house?

An engaging personality is inherent in this extraordinary color. Try this approach to making your home both unusual and attractive. Landscape with lots of evergreens and coordinating colors such as violet and blue.

Housebody color:	1. Benjamin Moore—Pink Petals 2085-60
Trim color:	2. Benjamin Moore—Brilliant White
Details:	3. Benjamin Moore—Gypsy Love 2085-30 on door and details
	4. Benjamin Moore—Old Pickup Blue 2054-60

For a Different Look

Use colors from the existing recipe, and decide which colors to emphasize by featuring them on the architectural elements of your choice. For instance, you might choose a white door and colored trim rather than the white trim and a colored door.

Perfectly Painted:

Choose two or three colors to accentuate the details on a particularly interesting

element, such as a carving. You could, for instance, use a darker shade of a single

color on the underside or flat part of the surface to emphasize the depth of the carving.

Farmhouse Red Darkest Berry

I saw the spiders marching through the air,

swimming from tree to tree that mildewed day

In latter August when the hay

Came creaking to the barn... .

—Robert Lowell, "Mr. Edwards and the Spider"

The settling of America was a utopian adventure for many Europeans. It was a new beginning, yet they brought their color sense with them. This was reflected in the paint colors used on their homes. Colonial settlers were dependent on imported blocks of dried pigment for these colors. They were expensive, so most homeowners, especially those in rural areas, relied on local colors ground from the earth, plants, and berries. This explains why red houses seem to organically blend with their environments.

This red house is painted in keeping with these historic origins. The simple split rail fence adds interest to this rustic home.

Consider your house. Is it clapboard or shingle? Such traditional red looks best on clapboard. What size is your home? If too large a surface area is painted red, the effect will become overwhelming. Complement the main portion of the house with neutral elements on smaller sections of the house, such as shake shingling or stone on the garage or breezeway. In this case, where the main portion of the house is of moderate size, there is no denying red looks great.

Perfectly Painted:

Generally speaking, the less complex the trimming on a house, the fewer colors you will use.

Housebody and trim color:	1. California Paints—Roasted Pepper AC116N
Details:	2. California Paints—Old Porch 8636N

For a Different Look

The door color in this recipe is subdued. You can bring more color into this scheme simply by painting the door green rather than this charcoal color. A green door is a less restrained, more colorful alternative.

Pink
Surprise Dusty Pink

The essential elements...of the romantic spirit are curiosity and the love of beauty.

—Walter Pater

This house is an appealing combination of dusty pink, gray, and cream. The colors bring an element of surprise and sparkle to the neighborhood. Notice that the stairs, window frames, and some decorative detailing echo the gray of the roof shingle. This is appropriate, given that the shingle is itself decorative. Cream trim frames and highlights the pink and gray. Green foliage complements and softens the hard lines of the house.

This dusty pink is gentle and muted. It is sophisticated, upscale, and even romantic. The gray detailing keeps it looking grounded. Even if your home does not feature such intricate detailing, this combination of colors could play up those interesting elements that are present.

If you are a plant lover, get out your garden tools. The color pink has been shown to influence the growth of plants. Plants grown in pink hothouses actually grow twice as fast and are sturdier than those grown in blue hothouses.

Housebody color:	1. Sherwin-Williams—Pink Prelude SW2295
Trim color:	2. Sherwin-Williams—Classical White SW2829
Details:	3. Sherwin-Williams—Tricorn Black SW2126 on details and door trim
	4. Sherwin-Williams—Stonecutter SW2124 on door and trim details
	5. Sherwin-Williams—Roseroot SW2711 on trim details

For a Different Look
Try using the trim color from this recipe, Rosewood, on the door. It will give the house more sparkle without changing the color scheme at all.

Perfectly Painted:

Paint carved wooden details with one main color and up to three accent colors.

Rustic Red Barn Red

The wilderness provides that perfect relaxation which all jaded minds require.

—William H. H. Murrays

Normally, we think of red as a color that packs a punch—that jumps out at us and excites. This red house is anything but that. Instead, it exemplifies the height of serenity and calm. This is partly due to the choice of red—a deep brick color—and also a result of pairing the color with natural wood and other natural, neutral elements.

This red is great on houses with shingles or wood clapboard. To ensure that it feels restful and interesting, be sure to use a combination of materials. Include natural wood in the color scheme. For example, you might include a wooden porch, deck, or staircase, and gravel or pea-stone paths and driveway.

This house is extraordinarily special because it incorporates actual trees in the architecture—as columns on the porch. Red painted trim on the porch door also enlivens the look. Window trim can be painted red or green, as seen here.

Your house doesn't need to have these embellishments to be attractive in red. This paint color will work on the most ordinary house. Keep the landscaping simple—greens with a few hints of color.

The wonder of this house is how ingeniously a rather ordinary structure is at once made to feel contemporary and rustic.

Housebody and trim color:	1. Benjamin Moore—Heritage Red
Details:	natural wood and green trim on windows

For a Different Look

For an even more rustic, woodsy look, you can eliminate the green window trim, and instead use the Heritage Red house body color on the window trim. For a hint of contrast and some added interest, use green paint on the door frame. The house will maintain its warm, serene quality.

Music Man

Creamy Pink

A songwriter is really a journalist of the time with music. —Edgar Yipsel Harburg

Here is the quintessential example of Americana—a neat and tidy, creamy Victorian house with white trim. It conjures up images of *The Music Man*—you can almost imagine folks strolling down perfectly manicured streets, eating ice cream cones on a sunny summer day.

The color of the house is highlighted with the addition of pale pink gingerbread cutout shingles, dashes of red on the flag, and hanging potted geraniums. The neutral gray steps and porch maintain a soft look.

As for details, you can keep it simple, like this homeowner did, by sporting a natural wood door—or, for a more dazzling effect, you can paint the door—not the screen door) a vibrant red or orange, or a lovely blue, framed with white moldings. This will give the house a much more playful and dynamic look.

The landscaping is monochrome green. A neutral background is capable of sustaining all the colors of the rainbow. So you can get as creative as you wish with your choice of affinity and landscape colors.

Housebody color:	1. Benjamin Moore—Odessa Pink HC-60 on gingerbread-style shingles; natural stain on door
Trim color:	2. Benjamin Moore—White

For a Different Look
Nothing is friendlier than a bright blue-, wild cherry-, or tangerine-colored door. All of these color choices make this house a more welcoming house. Depending on the shade that you choose, a colored door can add an otherwise absent air of whimsy.

Perfectly Painted:

If you have a textured house, the color you paint over it can make

the texture seem more or less apparent; choose carefully.

Red Detailing

Do you love red but worry about painting the whole house? You can get enormous impact from red even if you only use it on the doors, the trim, or on decorative elements, such as benches that have been placed beside the house. Here are a few striking samples.

Left:
Feel the excitement that red elicits on this otherwise neutral shingled home. If you prefer an earthy color for your house but wish to create a dynamic, exciting facade, consider painting the trim red. This bold crimson commands your attention without upsetting the down to earth quality of this home.

Above:
Red accents on this cobalt blue panel add interest and life, while drawing attention to the faux-marble finish and touches of gold. Consider this treatment to make a house sparkle.

Left:
The entrance to this West Coast Victorian comes to life with some well-placed splashes of deep cranberry. The red, white, and dark blue details become the focal point on a soothing gray background.

The triumphant colorist

has only to appear. We have prepared his

palette for him. —Paul Signac

Orange is the sunset, finely finished wood, sherbet, the center of a squash, a roaring fire, and a hillside in autumn. We are mesmerized by the sight of it. We all love peach, coral, salmon, gold, and amber.

When you imagine an orange house, a home in Santa Fe may come to mind. Perhaps your imagination travels to the warm climates of the Mediterranean or Mexico. But you needn't feel limited by your location. Orange also works in any locale, bringing sunny, tranquil luminosity to a home.

Chances are, if you choose to paint your house orange, you are good-natured with a bright disposition, adventurous, and enthusiastic. Don't worry about blending in; orange ties in well with the landscape colors of all four seasons.

Orange can feel startling if not chosen properly. These recipes are good guidelines for choosing subtle shades. The safest oranges are in either the deeper shades of orange-brown or the gentler, paler tints, such as peach, apricot, and cantaloupe.

Venture into this new territory when thinking about color. Adorned with orange, your home will be a splendid, radiating jewel in the afternoon light.

Radiant
Orange Bright, Dynamic

The dreams which accompany all human actions should be nurtured

by the places in which people live. —Charles W. Moore

Who says you can't paint your house orange? Just look at this stunning example. What a wonderful case of a standard box-style Colonial turned into a show house simply with paint. And to think, Americans have used this color on exteriors since this Essex, Massachusetts house was built in 1730. Orange attracts us like a magnet. Turn your somber house into a stunning attention-getter.

If you prefer a more dressed-up home, add paneled shutters painted a deep gloss green or red. Paint the front door the same color and add a natural wood stained storm door over it. Plain or dressy, this friendly orange house will brighten anyone's day.

Housebody color:	1. Pittsburgh Paints—Buffalo Trail 219-5
Trim color:	2. Pittsburgh Paints—Super White 88-45
Details:	3. Pittsburgh Paints—Walnut Grove 511-7 on door

For a Different Look

A high-gloss forest green or chrome red door will dress up this house without changing its simplicity. For added elegance, take this one step further—add shutters, and paint them the same color as the door.

Perfectly Painted:

Add a band of contrasting color along the roofline to bring out the shape of the house.

Song of the Broad Axe

Soft, Creamy Pale Apricot

The house-builder at work...the preparatory jointing, squaring, sawing, mortising, the hoist-up of

beams, the push of them in their places, laying them regular, setting the studs by their tenons in

the mortises according as they were prepared, the blows of mallets and hammers, the attitudes

of the men, their curv'd limbs, bending, standing astride the pins, holding on by posts and braces,

the hook'd arm over the plate, the other arm wielding the axe...their postures bringing their

weapons downward on the bearers, the echoes resounding. —Walt Whitman, "Song of a Carpenter"

Few architectural styles offer the elegant simplicity of the eighteenth-century New England home, which is modest in design, uncomplicated, and stark. This circa 1750 pale apricot house with yellow trimmings glows with warmth, even on the drabbest winter days. It stands in contrast to the leafless tree limbs of winter that encompass it and offers warmth against the frequent white snows. Orange and yellow blend naturally with autumn's colors and complement the lush green foliage of spring and summer—great color choices for any time of year.

This particular orange paint color flies in the face of tradition. White-washing was the earliest form of house painting in America. However, by the mid-eighteenth century, American paint makers were mixing a wide range of colors. Yellow and umber were among the most commonly used.

This house has few fixed features. Those that exist are neutral and need not be considered in the overall color scheme. Plantings are sparse and also neutral. The pale apricot paint color is what makes this home striking. It is just unusual enough to grab your attention, yet subtle, so the simplicity of the property is retained.

The ever-changing daylight plays on this pale color and ensures a handsome start and finish to every day.

		1		2		3

Housebody color: 1. Benjamin Moore—Asbury Sand 2156-50

Trim colors: 2. Benjamin Moore—Montgomery White

Details: 3. Benjamin Moore—Black on doors

For a Different Look

For more visual interest, try a colored door rather than black.
Deep green or red tones work nicely with the apricot house body
color. Either color would add sparkle to this house.

California Contemporary

Dusty Orange

Architecture must have integrity, like a friend. —I. M. Pei

This stunning contemporary stucco residence is marvelous in orange. Gray columns and multiple neutral architectural elements lead the eye from the house to the threshold of nature. Colors and textures combine to make a successful whole.

This strongly linear building, which might have appeared stark in gray or white, is instead made a lively work of art by brilliant orange and violet-gray. Orange is intensified by sunlight and is dramatic against a bright blue sky. The choice of violet-gray or blue-gray is drawn from the undertones of stone and cement. Thin black trim is used to accentuate windows. Should you prefer to play down contrast, you could use white instead. This combination, however, makes the most of complementary colors, architectural features, and harmony with nature.

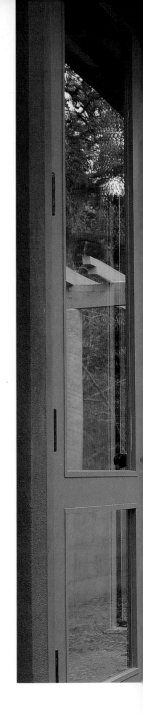

Housebody color:	1. California Paints—Glazed Carrot 7326A
Trim color:	2. California Paints—Pretty Purple 7973M
Details:	California Paints—Pretty Purple 7973M on doors;
	3. Black on window frames

For a Different Look

For a more colorful, daring look, consider a deep indigo blue or violet as your trim and door color. The existing gray doors and trim on this house merely hint at violet. Using deep, dark shades of violet will have a greater impact without changing the overall subtlety of the look of the house.

Perfectly Painted:

Accent a window by combining two colors—one on the sash and one on the trim.

Orange Detailing

Do you love orange but worry about painting the whole house? Orange makes a bold and welcoming statement even if used only sparingly. Perhaps consider orange just for the front door. Here are a few examples of orange detailing.

Above:
Orange is less intense than red and has more of the sunny qualities of yellow. Hot and luminous, orange is a gregarious, extrovert-
ed front door color. Coupled with this cool, turquoise porch, it
makes for a nicely balanced but dramatic and soulful entrance.
This combination of colors is reminiscent of the autumn harvest—
blue October skies, brown and burnt orange. What a friendly welcome to a deep, dark brown house. This is an adventurous color
statement for the assertive homeowner.

Left:
Orange trim keeps this Victorian from blending in with the crowd,
and its vibrant color scheme really pops. While it may be overwhelming for some people, attention-getting orange can be a
great choice for the vivacious extroverts among us.

Yellow

Oh, what a beautiful mornin'

Oh, what a beautiful day.

I got a beautiful feelin'

Everything's going my way.

—Oscar Hammerstein II, from *Oklahoma!*

Yellow is seen by many as the happiest of all colors. If you are thinking of painting your house yellow, you are probably warm and optimistic, with a sunny disposition. Yellow creates an instantly cheerful and sunny family greeting. It is the perfect color for lifting spirits and, therefore, an excellent choice for climates with many gray days.

Consider the use of these yellows if your house is shingle, wood, or aluminum siding—buttery or creamy yellow, canary yellow, mellow amber yellow, even mustard yellow. Yellow is also seen on stucco houses in Florida and California, where the styles are often Spanish hacienda, Mediterranean, and Italian villa.

Yellow is an especially friendly front door color. Just imagine a dazzling lemon-yellow door and gleaming white trim on a rainy day. A yellow door is a great treatment for cedar shake or natural shingle houses. Picture sparkling chrome-yellow shutters on a white clapboard house. What a great accent! How about a golden yellow house with red trim? Or emerald-green trim on a bright yellow farmhouse to tie the building into its surrounding landscape?

Yellow is one of the most versatile colors for homes of any style and in any climate. And there are so many possibilities to choose from. To avoid a yellow oops, follow the guidelines in the recipes that follow. For the skittish, yellow is the safest color choice outside the neutrals.

Housebody color:	1. Benjamin Moore—Cream Yellow 2155-60
Trim color:	2. Benjamin Moore—Dove White
Details:	3. Benjamin Moore—Black on door and shutters

For a Different Look

You can create more color interest by adding red shutters. This is a bold statement and will change the character of the house, so be sure to test your red on one or two sets of shutters before painting them all. Another attractive treatment, and one that will not change the character of the house, is to paint the door and shutters a pleasant shade of green—you decide how light or dark.

Village Home

Butter Cream

The days are short, the weather's cold, by tavern fires tales are told.

—New England Almanac, Dec. 1704

Imagine strolling into town on a still winter day, passing pretty home after pretty home, many dating to the 1700s and 1800s. Icicles hang over the eaves. Shrubs and rooftops are dusted with snow. Leafless maple and oak trees filter the light. You are approaching a quaint and charming village where you plan to stop for a cup of hot tea and reflect on your day.

This yellow village home has the charm of a bygone era and the clean lines of a brand new house. It was built at the turn of the century—the twenty-first century, that is. It sits on a small lot with limited frontage on a busy road close to the village center. It is stunning in its architectural simplicity, and the paint colors chosen for it couldn't be more suitable. Decorative embellishments, such as brass fixtures on the front door and the festive holiday fruit decoration over it, add elegance to this sweet home.

This yellow is moderately vivid. It seems brighter in contrast with the high-gloss black shutters and door. The fixed features are the neutral granite steps and walk. This recipe works equally well with brick walk and steps. Green foliage with pink, magenta, and white blossoms is particularly beautiful against the background of this yellow house.

Winter Solstice Bright Chrome Yellow

Snow...makes one think not of a clean slate, a glorious future, but of a happy past and never mind that the past never really was like that. —Paul Goldberger

The Colonial house has been a fixture of residential architecture in America since the arrival of the first European settlers. A two-story clapboard box with a center chimney, this classic yellow Colonial is like countless homes of today seen in virtually every area of the country. It is a representative sample.

What makes this home distinctive is its brilliant yellow color, which resonates against a bright blue sky or bright white snow. Gloss black shutters heighten the effect. A chrome-yellow house is an especially welcome site on a dark night when lit from the outside. Yellow is compatible with virtually all colors that typically surround a house, making it a suitable paint color choice for your Colonial during any season. This home has classic, simple shrubs and evergreens. During spring and summer, potted flowers add color to the front facade. Brick walks and the neutral driveway are subtle and relatively unnoticeable.

Make your Colonial home special. Set it apart from all others with your paint color choice. Consider this wonderful yellow and enjoy its cheerfulness all year round. You may choose to paint shutters black or green and highlight the front door with still another color. Use your creativity.

1 2 3

Housebody color:	1. California Paints Historic Colors of America—Pale Organza
Trim color:	2. California Paints—White
Details:	3. California Paints—Black

For a Different Look

Dark green shutters make a traditional yellow house even more traditional. Perhaps you prefer this look over black shutters on this house. For a more dynamic, less traditional look, try a nice red on the shutters. Regardless of the shutter color, you can leave the door color black if desired.

Perfectly Painted:

Classic architectural styles lend themselves to classic combinations, such as this yellow house paint combined with gloss black on shutters.

Golden Yellow

Rich, Mellow Gold

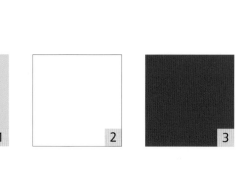

On entering some of our villages, the only color which meets the eye is white.

Everything is white; the houses, the fences, the stables, the kennels, and sometimes

even the trees cannot escape, but get a coat of white wash…Is this taste? Whether

it be or not, one thing is certain, that a great change is coming over our people in

this respect. They are beginning to see that there are beauties in color as well as form.

—Samuel Sloan, 1852

This cozy shingled home is adorable painted all in gold. The color has a rich, burnished quality. The house projects a modest dignity. A dark red painted chimney and freshly whitewashed picket fence complete this charming residence.

The color is at once complex and natural. It is the color of Mother Earth, essentially ocher, which is associated with substance and stability. Variations in light transform this golden ocher into shades of cinnamon, honey, and ecru. The home emits a sense of simplicity, comfort, hearth, and family roots.

All year around, this house just glows. Keep accompanying landscape colors subdued—primarily green foliage and white blossoms. Brick and stone create an even more grounded and ordered look.

1   2   3

Housebody color:	1. Benjamin Moore—Dorset Gold HC-8
Trim:	2. Benjamin Moore—White
Details:	3. Benjamin Moore—Heritage Red 25 on chimney; Benjamin Moore—White on fence

For a Different Look

Try a lovely dark burgundy color on the doors. Make it a deep purple-red. This adds depth and richness to the existing color scheme.

Farmhouse Yellow Medium Lemon Yellow

One day in the country is worth a month in town. —Christina Rossetti

Spring is beautiful in New England. This soft yellow farmhouse casts a warm glow and lives harmoniously in nature. The basic palette is yellow on the house accompanied by an old peeling red on the barn. Notice the green roof, which contributes to the sense of balance, as red is green's complement.

Whether or not your roof is green, consider farmhouse yellow for your clapboard house. It shines within its surroundings and has a hearty quality that sustains its appearance through the chilly depths of winter. Landscape colors may be chosen freely because this palette is so neutral. This color is a classic. Keep the promise of spring alive with this yellow choice.

Housebody color:	1. Benjamin Moore—Light Yellow 2022-60
Trim color:	2. Benjamin Moore—White Dove
Details:	Benjamin Moore—White Dove on doors

For a Different Look

For an uplifting appearance, paint the doors blue—either a light or dark shade. Blue doors will connect the house its surroundings—a vast blue sky. As an alternative to blue, green doors make a nice but more traditional statement.

Perfectly Painted:

Lighter paint colors give a more reflective, brighter appearance.

Housebody color:	1. Sherwin-Williams—Yellow Corn SW2348
Trim color:	2. Sherwin-Williams—Chicory SW2035
Details:	Sherwin-Williams—Chicory SW2035 on door

For a Different Look

Blue is a beautiful color choice for the trim and doors of this adobe, either the blue color of twilight—a pale periwinkle—or a deep azure, midnight blue. A blue with an electric quality is always enlivening.

Adobe Yellow

Ocher

The earth is an Indian thing. —Jack Kerouac

It is no surprise that this golden ocher yellow has special significance in many cultures as symbolic of the sun. In Japan, it is considered the color of heaven.

The color alone gives this house a strong presence. Here, it is offset by the brickwork and brown beams. In the Southwest, where these warm hues predominate, you can add bright orange, cobalt blue, or purple as a trim color, but you can use this yellow in any part of the country on stucco surfaces. If your region doesn't warrant contrasting bright colors as part of the house color scheme, introduce additional colors in planters or within the landscaping. This will provide a stunning embellishment to the house color. Notice the power of black on details such as ironwork. Ocher and black seem meant for each other.

1

2

Perfectly Painted:

To highlight the brick front of a house, use a contrasting color such as yellow on the housebody or on details such as shutters.

Deep Gold

This home in the New England vernacular, with its elegant symmetry, is saturated in thick layers of earthy yellow paint. When applying a bold color, confidence is everything. Unfortunately, risk is an essential element in this often anxiety-provoking process. But looking at the rich facade of this old house, you realize the risk is worthwhile. This heavy color cries out for lightness to provide balance. In the absence of additional colors on the housebody, the white picket fencing is the brightening solution. The sparkling white frames the yard and home.

Gold, the color of changing foliage, provides warmth in winter and sunshine in the spring. Your house need not be a historic landmark to be outfitted in this palette. However, architectural simplicity that lets the color be the star is best.

Freely add color within the landscape. You don't need to limit yourself to green.

Housebody colors:	1. Benjamin Moore—Roasted Sesame Seed 2160-40
Trim colors:	Benjamin Moore—Buttercup 2154-30
Details:	2. Benjamin Moore—Acadia White AC-41 on window sashes

For a Different Look
To brighten this yellow house, paint the door white. Or, for a more sedate look, paint the door black.

Yellow Detailing

Do you love yellow but worry about painting the whole house? You can get the warmth and friendliness of yellow by incorporating it into paneled carvings and architectural elements such as pillars, trim, or doors. Here are a few examples to consider.

Left:
Yellow is a splendid choice for highlighting the many wonderful details on this blue Victorian. It emits a friendly, happy, even playful mood. Yellow helps make the house more cheerful and warm, too. Accompanying white trim frames the house and draws people in. The addition of this white trim helps to lighten the heft of the house. Yellow and blue alone would create a heavier look.

Opposite, top:
Sunny yellow trim adds warmth and light to the front porch of this Queen Anne row house. Because yellow is a high-reflection color, it advances to the eye, making it a stand-out trim color for any house whose features or lines you would like to accentuate. It would not be the best color choice for a home without details you wish to highlight.

Right:
This carved wooden door detail is truly enhanced with the simple addition of gold-leaf paint. The fan shape, with its glimmering golden rays, gives the whole house a real lift. This is a very easy way to bring a sparkle to your home. Treat the details on your front door with a highlighting color. Even if the entire house and door are painted the same color, you can still add personality and a warm welcome with a splash of golden yellow.

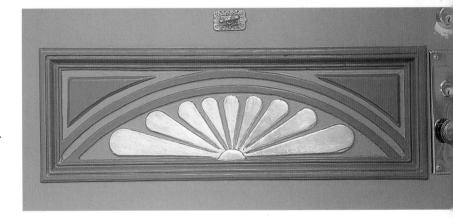

Green

It's not that easy bein' green.

—Joe Raposo, "Bein' Green," sung by Kermit the Frog

It's true; green is not the most popular exterior paint color. You may be hesitant to paint your house green for fear that it will look like a giant lime or a Crayola crayon. But don't worry. This section will change the way you think about green. These recipes are tried and true.

Nature put more greens on earth than any other color—thousands of variations on emerald, chartreuse, pine, sage, and olive. Green is about renewal, hope, life, and fertility.

Consider giving your home a new life with seafoam, a soft, pale green perfect in both northern and southern climates, and trimming it in cream. The palest tints of blue-green, such as aquamarine and turquoise, evoke distant images of the placid Aegean Sea. Moss-green siding is perfect with crisp white window frames.

Want a dramatic change? Decorate your red brick house with a wintergreen door, shutters, and window boxes. Or paint the accent moldings of your weathered shingle house in vibrant green and sunny yellow to completely brighten and freshen the look.

If you are inclined to paint your house green, chances are you are a stable, balanced, social person. Enjoy entertaining in a home wrapped in nature's most popular hue.

The Frog Prince Bright Emerald

The eye experiences a distinctly grateful impression from

this color. —Goethe

Modest Victorian houses of no distinct style are found across the country. This bright green house, with its crisp white trim, does not reflect nineteenth-century painting practices. It was not customary to paint the entire house one color, nor to have the cornice, corner boards, and window and door frames in stark contrast. However, the choice of this particular green was the perfect way to turn this frog into a prince. This green has a clean, fresh quality that shines within the surrounding landscape.

Though simple, this house is a color showstopper. Green might be a wonderful color choice for your Victorian home too. You can avoid clashing with this green by landscaping with yellow.

Housebody color:	1. Benjamin Moore—Cedar Green 2034-40
Trim and door color:	2. Brilliant White

For a Different Look
A pale yellow on the front door would make this house more brilliant, sunny, and warm. For even more color, use the same yellow (as well as white) in the carved designs, on the window frames, and along the eaves.

Eternally Green Deep Blue-Green

On a gray day it will look like a moth; on a sunny day like a butterfly. —Louis I. Kahn

The strength of this contemporary mission-style bungalow lies in its choice of building materials, its geometry, and its paint colors. Its style is rendered less common by unusual choices—in color, of deep blue-green, and of varying sizes of clapboards, shingles, and heavy concrete columns. Varnished wooden window frames take on an orange glow and brighten the serious edge of a rather somber green house.

Charcoal-gray detailing complements the cream-colored patio and architectural elements and introduces yet another color. The house feels grounded and earthy, yet is enlivened with multiple details.

This blue-green is unobtrusive. It blends well with the outdoor environment and is an especially handsome choice. It combines color qualities of the sky and of the foliage and doesn't compete with either. Green is the most restful color to the eye.

To enliven your surroundings, landscape with lots of color—yellow iris, purple pansies, pink azaleas, orange daylilies and marigolds, and white bleeding heart.

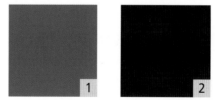

1   2   3

Housebody color:	1. Benjamin Moore—Casco Bay 2051-30
Trim color:	2. Benjamin Moore—Witching Hour 2120-30
Details:	3. Benjamin Moore—Moonlight White 2143-60 on columns; orange-tone stain and varnish on window frames

For a Different Look

For a smashing effect, try a deep cobalt blue on the doors. It is more dramatic than the existing green and gives the house a dreamy quality. Paint all the window frames pumpkin orange.

Camp House

Forest Green

To invite a person into your house is to take charge of his happiness for as long as he is under your roof. —Anthelme Brillat-Savarin

This forest green reminds me of the great outdoors. It has a strong and stable quality, much like the tall pines surrounding it. Charming and casual, the house has a laid-back kind of elegance.

Green is known as the great harmonizer by Indian mystics, to whom it represents the balance and harmony found in nature. This house, with its green color, does convey a sense of calm and of balance. Although it is dark, the color is still neutral and subtle.

The color chosen for this house allows a large, expensive home to take on an air of modesty—a camp quality. The house, its surroundings, and its colors are strangely dramatic in their serenity.

Landscaping should be done as though nature did it herself.

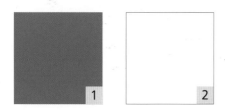

Housebody color:	1. Sherwin Williams—Mown Grass SW 2377
Trim color:	2. Sherwin Williams—White SW 2123

For a Different Look
Try incorporating more color into this scheme. Simply paint the door a lovely silvery, blueberry blue. The added interest will amaze you.

Perfectly Painted:

To make a house blend into its surroundings, avoid colors that contrast with those surroundings.

Victorian Sage Pale, Silvery Gray-Green

My salad days, when I was green in judgment.

—William Shakespeare, *Antony and Cleopatra*

This pale, silvery gray-green reminds me of the lovely shimmering perennial called lamb's ear. It has a soft and delicate quality. Overall, the house has a neutral, sophisticated, subtle color palette that emits a sort of luminescence. The palest green is strengthened with darker green and gray and highlighted with white trim. Wooden gingerbread fretwork brings a jaunty quality to this house, an air of frivolity.

Your house may not have this much detailing. It may not even be a Victorian, but that doesn't mean you can't accentuate its positives using these colors. Green is the primary color, with white for detailing. Throw in a pinch of violet (as here, on the stained glass windows) for fun.

A large blossoming tree in green's complementary color (red) balances out the home perfectly.

Housebody color: 1. California Paints Historic Color—
Glenhaven 8134M

Trim color: 2. California Paints—Beach Basket 7750W

Details: 3. California Paints—Shaded Moss 8136N

For a Different Look

How about adding a pale violet-blue door? This color of lilac blossoms combined with the green house body color is reminiscent of the fresh colors of spring.

Green Detailing

Do you love green but worry about painting the whole house? You can get the pleasure of green even if you use it only sparingly on the doors or the detailing. Here are just a few examples.

Below:
Most greens are associated with the earth as the color of vegetation. But blue-green is more closely associated with the cool, refreshing ocean. On this building, blue-green is unobtrusive, blending in with the outdoor environment. It doesn't compete with the landscape, yet it adds a slight sparkle to its restful surroundings. If your goal is to create a sophisticated, upscale, soothing and fresh look for your house with only a splash of color, try blue-green.

Above:

There is an enormous range of green colors. This green is similar to the greens found in nature. In choosing this color, the house immediately becomes linked to its surroundings. Even with green trim, this house is neutral, because green is nature's neutral—the colors of foliage and growing plants. Green brings a sense of balance and harmony to this home.

Blue

...[A]s readily as we follow

an agreeable object that flies from us so we love to contemplate

blue, not because it advances to us, but because it draws us

after it. —Goethe, *Theory of Colors*

Blue is America's favorite color. Perhaps this is because blue suggests images of the sky and the sea, vast and serene. In truth, the brain's response to blue is relaxation. If you are contemplating painting your house blue, chances are it has always been your favorite color. You probably aspire to harmony, peace, perseverance, patience, and tranquility.

Blue is a dependable choice. Blue houses create a sense of coolness on a hot summer day and a rich, welcome contrast to white winter snow. Autumn provides the perfect complement (orange) to a blue domain.

Pale or light blue houses, like powder blue and Wedgwood blue, feel retiring, quiet and soothing, while deeper indigo blues, like cobalt and marine, come alive to offer a dramatic contrast to nature's colors. Flower-filled beds and bushes with blooms are even lovelier against the richness and timelessness of glorious blue.

Vivid indigo or cornflower blue houses make bold statements when paired with tangerine-orange or lime-green doors. For a traditional look, try black on the shutters and white on all the trim, or select a soft blue with off-white trim and yellow shutters for a more country feel. Pale blue shutters on a deeper blue house work well when coupled with black window frames and door. Change the look of stucco instantly with vivid azure blue accents. Aqua makes tan stucco look polished rather than drab. Blue houses seem to soar skyward, for they have a celestial quality. Enjoy the range of blue choices in these recipes.

Perfectly Painted:

Subtler colors can be emphasized by using their complement

or analogous colors on shutters, doors, etc. (see Appendix A).

Country Blue

Pale Blue-Gray

If you love me (but not quite),

Send me a ribbon, a ribbon of white.

If you love me, love me true,

Send me a ribbon, a ribbon of blue. —Nursery rhyme

Pale blue adds interest and charm to this country house, particularly because it is nestled between many white houses. Crisp white trim, red doors, and pale gray shutters give the house a neat and tidy finish. The house is accentuated by the emerald lawn in the foreground and the accompanying colorful palette of flowers.

This lovely paint treatment works as well on clapboard as it does on shake and shingles. Consider including lush greenery and adding brilliance with colorful flowers. Multicolored and white blossoms, especially reds, pinks, and purples, can be planted in profusion.

Unembellished homes can often be made to have as much presence as houses with applied decoration simply with paint.

This paint color suggests a sense of peace and tranquility.

Housebody color:	1. Sherwin-Williams—Skyway Blue SW2263
Trim color:	2. Sherwin-Williams White
Details:	3. Sherwin-Williams—Canal Blue SW2261 on shutters
	4. Sherwin-Williams—Elderberry SW 2902 on doors

For a Different Look

How about a pink door? It doesn't have to be bright pink. It can be a subtle, grayed pink. The color would be an uplifting, friendly addition to this blue house. Consider substituting blue shutters for the existing gray shutters. Find a fairly deep shade of blue that appeals to you. This color combination will transform your traditional house to a quaint and charming home with a touch of whimsy.

Slate Dark Slate Blue

A man possessed by peace never stops smiling. —Milan Kundera

Here is a stunning example of the enormous impression a dark color can make on the appearance of a house. This historic blue home appears formal and serious, tranquil and peaceful. Imagine if this house were painted all white, or a light color. It would present an altogether completely different mood for the viewer.

Notice that the trim is painted the same color as the house. With so little color contrast, the house feels stayed and grounded. A burgundy door provides the only break in color and adds some warmth. A short, delicate white fence lightens the heaviness of the house.

If you like dark, historic colors, and your clapboard house has simple, straightforward lines without a lot of detailing, you may be able to use this recipe. Keep your landscaping low. You can certainly add more color within your plantings. Notice the impact of the light wisps of pale-colored perennials and consider adding them into your landscape.

Perfectly Painted:

Dark paint colors don't show dirt as easily as light colors do.

Housebody color:	1. Benjamin Moore—Hamilton Blue 36
Trim color:	Benjamin Moore—Hamilton Blue 36
Details:	2. Benjamin Moore—Cherokee Brick 2082-30

For a Different Look
Consider a black door rather than a burgundy red door. It will not change the character of the house. Rather, it makes an already well-groomed home appear even more formal.

Perfectly Painted:

*Use a contrasting color to paint around the outside edge
of all the window and door frames to create visual interest
and unify the overall design.*

Gloucester Victorian Blue-Gray

Come in the evening, come in the morning. Come when expected, come without warning; Thousands of welcomes you'll find here before you, and the oftener you come, the more we'll adore you. —Irish rhyme

Check out the interesting combination of blues on this unusual Victorian house. Blue-gray clapboards are toned down by the slightly more intense blue door and window sashes. A bravura splash of warm yellow trim and gold detailing creates an eye-popping contrast and makes the blue on the house feel as cool as a cucumber.

Can you use these colors on your house? Yes, easily. Simply apply the colors to your ranch house, bungalow, cape or beach house. Blue-gray is great on clapboards, but also works on shingles and even on stucco. Gold can be used as an accent color on wooden house details.

The vivid colors used on the house, and its inherent architectural interest, make a strong statement without the need for any major landscaping. A few low-growing greens and pretty annuals or perennials will add softness to the hard lines of the architecture. Keep the look casual, perhaps in the style of a cottage garden.

Housebody color:	1. Benjamin Moore Historic Colors—Whipple Blue HC-152
Trim color:	2. Benjamin Moore—Hepplewhite Ivory HC-36
Details:	3. Benjamin Moore—Deep Ocean 2058-30 on doors and window sashes
	4. Benjamin Moore—Chestertown Buff HC-9 on wooden details

For a Different Look

Try using the existing colors in this recipe, but on different parts of the house. For instance, you could use the house body color on the window sashes. This allows you to emphasize the colors you want without changing the color scheme or stylistic details. Consider using a different color on the doors. Red or gold are great options.

Pale Blue-Gray Cottage

There are fairies at the bottom of our garden!

—Rose Fyleman

This lovely blue bungalow house is illuminated by the May morning sun. It glows during daytime hours and, in the evening, seems almost to vibrate with color, giving the house a magical quality. Its Gothic windows and deeper blue trim heighten the effect. Gentle white dogwood blossoms and natural splashes of violet azalea and rhododendron enliven it further. This color is alive, yet calming. Green foliage provides a lush surrounding and ties the dreamlike house to reality.

If you love blue and have a shingled, stucco, or clapboard cape, ranch, or bungalow, this may be just the color palette for you. It is enchanting without being shocking or overly fanciful. This is a color that demands special attention. Your house will surely draw interest, having an aura of mystery and intrigue.

Housebody color:	1. California Paints—Basin Blue 7991W
Trim color:	2. California Paints—Wonder Blue 7524M
Details:	California Paints—Ocean Depths 8045D on inner windows

For a Different Look
Paint the front door white instead of blue—it will contemporize the house and give it a clean fresh look.

Blue Detailing

Do you love blue but worry about painting the whole house? Bring the serenity of blue into your color scheme by painting only the shutters, trim, doors, or other house details. Here are a couple of examples.

Left:
What a knockout this charcoal house becomes with a cobalt blue door. With or without the bright yellow window trim, this house is awakened with cobalt blue. Vivid, brilliant blue is electrifying. It energizes the entire house and lends a welcoming, playful quality. Deeper blues have a meditative quality making it the perfect blue choice for this house set among tall pines in the forest.

Above:
Blue shutters add not merely color to this lovely Cape but create a mood of tranquility. The house seems to have a consoling spirit—not surprising since blue is felt to be a spiritually calming color. Gazing at this house produces a sense of contentment and relaxation. If you wish to create a peaceful, serene atmosphere, choose blue as your shutter color—and use it on the front door too.

Violet

The purest and most thoughtful

minds are those which love color the most. —John Ruskin

Whether a delicate mauve or deep plum, violet is sophisticated and can be highly success-ful as a house paint color.

We tend to think of violet as exotic because it was once the color reserved for roy-alty and is still the color of exotic blossoms and fruits. But violets come in an exciting array of shades from casual to chic. All are combinations of the primary colors blue and red.

Violet is generally considered a cool color. The bluer the violet, the more subdued, tranquil, and cool the color appears. The redder the violet, the more it advances to the eye and takes on red's stimulating, hot qualities. So, when you choose among violets, think in terms of its red or blue undertones as well as its lightness and brightness to achieve your desired effect. You will enjoy the character of lavender, plum, grape, opal, dark aubergine, and orchid and the wonders they work in sunlight.

Picture a run-of-the-mill house made distinctive with dusty purple-gray paint and parrot-green shutters. This bit of whimsy adds the necessary charm to make the house the quaintest on the street.

For a subtler look, try a blue-gray violet on the body of the house and cream and gray on trim and windows. This is a soft, clean look that freshens, brightens, and updates even the dingiest old house. It makes a bright backdrop for evergreen bushes, climbing vines, and beds of annuals or perennials.

If you love violet, you are probably highly creative, artistic, and sensitive as well as generous and charming. You aren't afraid to be different. The recipes that follow are chosen for folks from shy to adventurous.

Indigo

Here is a fearless paint color for you—a bright lilac purple. It brings this bungalow to life and draws us in. The house is punctuated by white trim and hints of yellow coreopsis.

With this paint color, an otherwise ordinary house becomes a cool oasis. If you dare to be bold and paint your house lilac purple, violet paint with white trim is all you really need. Notice that the porch balusters are painted in accents of blue for consistency and simplicity. Add dashes of color within the landscape.

Notice how the fixed features are neutral—cement walk, weathered wood fence. Thus, the house is truly the point of interest. You have the option of using green or red trim rather than white. These alternatives will work well but generate a camp or cabinlike feeling.

 1

 2

 3

 4

Housebody color:	1. Benjamin Moore—California Lilac 2068-40
Trim color:	2. Benjamin Moore—Brilliant White
Details:	3. Benjamin Moore—Bermuda Blue 2061-30
	4. Benjamin Moore—Dior Gray 2133-40

For a Different Look

Consider the use of green or red trim rather than white for a cabin-like feel. Or, use all the designated colors indicated in the recipe except the door color. Instead, paint the door red. This makes an already bold statement even more dynamic.

1

2

3

4

5

Regal Violet

Soothing Grape

Mid pleasures and palaces though we may roam,

Be it ever so humble, there's no place like home.

—J. Howard Payne, *Clari, the Maid of Milan*

This grape-colored Victorian is representative of the row-house style, seen from down the Mississippi, across the lower South, up the East Coast to New England, back to the Midwest, and out to the Rockies and the California coast, where it has gained much fame.

The soothing, lovely grape color and accompanying cobalt trim, combined with creamy off-white, gray-green, and violet detailing create an elegantly eclectic color mixture. The balanced facade is accentuated by the detailing on the portico pilasters, porch, and door. This is a stunning example of the regal quality that emanates from some tones of purple. The majestic, rich, interesting, and sophisticated quality of this home is due, in part, to its inherent architectural beauty, but also to the choices in paint colors.

Be careful with your selection of landscape colors. Simple evergreen foundation plantings with one or two potted flowers on the portico is all you really need.

Housebody color:	1. Benjamin Moore—Gentle Violet 2071-20
Trim:	2. Benjamin Moore—Navajo White
Details:	3. Benjamin Moore—Twilight Blue 2067-30 on trim; 4. Benjamin Moore—Misty Lilac 2071-70; 5. Benjamin Moore—Northampton Putty HC-89 on porch and door

For a Different Look
Simply use white paint on the porch and door for a lighter, crisper look.

Perfectly Painted:

Columns or pillars can be painted with one main color and up to three accent colors on carved parts.

Gillman Garrison House Plum

He best can paint them who shall feel them most.

—Alexander Pope

The color purple makes an exciting and memorable impact on the unpretentious honesty of a simple Colonial wood house. The Gillman Garrison House (c. 1690) was originally built as a fortified house to protect local sawmills. Who would guess? This New England house keeps its secrets behind plum-colored clapboards. A pale brown natural wooden door and white trim highlight the few ornamental moldings and doorways. The subtle purple and pink undertones in the red brick walk tie into the house color.

Purple is a wonderful and unusual color choice. Why settle for brown or even red when you can have this sophisticated, colorful plum? Does your home have simple, clean lines with few or no embellishments? Do you enjoy the minimalist look? These are the main criteria for using this paint color. The color itself provides all the interest you will need. It even negates the need to accessorize. Purple intrigues the eye in every landscape. Try it and see.

Housebody Color:	1. California Paints—Glorious Plum 8905D
Trim Color:	2. California Paints—White Solitude CW057W
Details:	Natural wood stained doors

For a Different Look

Some people prefer a painted front door. Think about the colors that you like, and then consider how they might work with purple. For instance, barn or cherry reds may not work well for you on this purple house. Black works with almost all colors. Green is great with purple. Some blues also work with purple. Orange would be extremely dramatic and bold. Experiment, and find your favorite.

Violet Detailing

Do you love violet but worry about painting the whole house? You can get added color interest using your creative touch and violet even if it is applied only to the doors, trim, or on other house details. Here are some wonderful examples.

Right:
Heather-toned violet-blue details cool down this yellow house and add a hint of refinement. It is a quiet and low-key color, making it a nice, serene choice for embellishing your Victorian.

Opposite, top:
Do you love violet but prefer not to paint it on the house? Then plant a wisteria and drape the entire front of your house in violet. The plant becomes a fixed feature on the house adding drama, character, and color during part of each year. Make a chocolate brown house extraordinary with masses of violet blossoms.

Right:
This whimsical, witty combination of accent colors brings a unique character to this little house. And, since people who prefer violet tend to be artists and nonconformists, it's no wonder that violet dominates the scheme. Included are a light and darker violet, with its complement, yellow, and a high impact berry red. The result is a wonderful combination of excitement and tranquility.

Violet is viewed by mystics as the color of spiritual intuition. Perhaps it was chosen for this reason, because in this landscape, the house seems to take on something of a mystical quality.

The Neutrals

White, Gray, Brown

... possess a sturdiness, a strong powerfulness which is not immediately evident. —B. J. Koumer, *Color Their Characters*

The word *neutral* is misleading because neutral colors run the gamut from pale tans, creams, and beige that only hint at color to deep umber browns, nutmegs, and dark gray. The range of color within the neutral spectrum is tremendous. Think of the difference between ivory and charcoal. Neutrals are elegant when contrasted with one another. White, brown, and black all exhibit both warmth and coolness depending on their companion or surrounding colors. They can be used with great success alongside bright or exotic colors, such as shocking pink or azure blue.

White

White is probably America's most common house color. Its popularity began in the Greek Revival era (c. 1830 – 1855) because of the mistaken impression that ancient Greeks lived in white buildings. (Golden Age Greek buildings were, in fact, bright and colorful.) Brilliant whites often have blue pigment added and are so bright they actually appear cool. Ivory, bone, parchment, and other off-whites are warmer choices. White reflects the light of the sunshine and the colors of its surroundings—the grass, the sky. White houses can be traditional or playful, depending on your use of colored trim and the style of your house. Imagine a white house with bright green trim the color of spring grass. Or red shutters and blue and white striped awnings for a nautical look. How about a white brick house with red trim and doors? A cream house with gray trim and a bright red-orange door has a stately look and a brilliantly welcoming entry. A combination of white and off-white is subtle but lively.

If you love white houses, you are probably neat and orderly. White shows form to its greatest advantage and is, therefore, great on contemporary homes, featuring their lines against grass and sky.

Gray

Gray is always a popular house paint color choice. It is nature's most perfect neutral and works well with every color of the rainbow. When placed next to another color, gray assumes a bit of that color's complement. Gray beside green seems slightly rosy. Gray beside orange takes on a bit of blue. Keep this in mind as you select trim and accent colors. Gray is especially wonderful on shingled houses, on clapboard homes, and for an old, weathered look. Gray-tinted stucco is pleasant. Whether charcoal, pearly, silvery, smoky, or pale, gray is dignified and conservative. Gray has a long-standing association with stone and rock—solid and strong. If you love gray, you are probably practical, calm, composed, and reliable.

Brown

Brown is down to earth, understated, rugged, and outdoorsy. It comes in a wide variety of popular choices for exteriors: brown sugar, coffee, cocoa, chocolate, cinnamon, light browns (like beige and tan), and taupe browns (gray-browns). Brown is a classic color. It is always understated and dignified. Picture Boston's brownstones and the Southwest's adobe brick houses. Brown is the perfect background for lively touches of color like red, blue, green, and white, which cheer its serious character. People who think they don't like brown often do love brown wood furnishings and floors. If you don't want a brown house, consider the lovely natural tones of a wood door. Those who favor brown have a down-to-earth love of simplicity and a reliable character.

Enjoy the colorful neutral recipes. You are sure to find one for your home sweet home.

Glowing
Gray Medium-Pale Putty Gray

Every branch big with it,

Bent every twig with it;

Every fork like a white web-foot;

Every street and pavement mute:

Some flakes have lost their way, and grope back upward, when

Meeting those meandering down they turn and descend again.

The palings are glued together like a wall,

And there is no waft of wind with the fleecy fall.

—Thomas Hardy, "Snow in the Suburbs"

Your doorbell rings. You open the door to the sounds of carolers dressed in colorful Christmas clothes, all bundled up in fuzzy hats, scarves, and mittens. There are children wearing wreaths of stars around their heads. It is a picture-perfect photo opportunity depicting *Home for the Holidays*. However, you don't need to live in snow country to enjoy this paint color recipe.

Every shade of gray is slightly different because each contains particles of many other colors. This putty gray is particularly stunning in winter, appearing luminous and glowing. The drama is created by pairing medium-pale gray with deeper gray shutters and contrasting it with white trim. House features become elegant silhouettes that attract the eye. For a greater sense of drama and formality, you can paint shutters black and consider a black door as well. While especially lovely in winter, this house has a depth and presence at any time of the year. Elegant, homey, and serene, this lovely gray and white color combination is a winning choice.

Housebody color:	1. California Paints—Phelps Putty
Trim color:	2. California Paints—Nu-White 4-7100
Details:	3. California Paints—Fieldstone on shutters

For a Different Look

There are a wide variety of grays that you might like on your shutters ranging from pewter tones to gray-greens. Don't feel limited by the gray provided with this recipe. Very deep green, almost black, is also a great shutter color on this gray house. A black door makes the classic accompaniment.

Gothic Beige Gray and Brown

As fair as morn, as fresh as May... —from a madrigal by John Wilbye

This gray and rosy-brown Gothic cottage with its natural stained wood door is elegant and warm. During the nineteenth century, the trim color would have been painted significantly darker than the house. Now, many homeowners prefer a subtler, smoother transition in color between the house and trim that is easier on the eye. For this reason, we often see white or off-white trim on these homes today, as evidenced here by the white trim detailing on the gable. Historically accurate colors are often viewed as too dark or drab and hold little appeal for today's homeowners.

This simple yet sophisticated palette looks equally as appealing on a Colonial Revival and on any of the smaller houses of the 1950s and 1960s—the split levels, ranches, and capes typically found in subdivisions. The color combination is effective on clapboard, shingle, and stucco houses as well. Any home with a cottage quality will look lovely in these colors. If you love the gray house body color, but not the rosey-brown trim, feel free to substitute it with a green or a violet color. Both alternative trim colors will change the mood of the house from warm to cool.

Foundation plantings are green with splashes of violet azalea and white hydrangea. Pale brick walks are completely neutral.

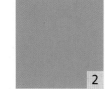

Housebody colors:	1. Benjamin Moore—Pink Beige SW2018
Trim colors:	2. Sherwin-Williams—Kashmir Sand SW2282
Details:	Natural wood door

For a Different Look
Violet-gray or green are great alternatives as door and trim colors.

White with a Twist

White, Cobalt Blue, and Yellow

Blow trumpet, for the world is white with May. —Alfred, Lord Tennyson

This white house is anything but neutral, with its yellow stars and blue shutters. The main house is plain white. Added to it are two tones of yellow and blue. What a stunning result! Granted, this house is an architectural jewel, but your white house can become something special too with colored detailing.

White houses are distinguished by their ability to reflect light. If you choose to paint your house white, why settle for traditional black or dark green shutters? Switch from prim to playful. While vibrant colors often do cause people to shy away in fear of making a color mistake, remember, it is just paint and can be easily altered. Try something dynamic—but be sure to test the colors on the house yourself before giving your painter the green light.

Don't let color scare you. For example, on a simple center-front Colonial, you could use blue on the shutters and two tones of yellow on a paneled front door. You would eliminate the natural wood all together. Or, perhaps, you have a Victorian. In this, case your options for color placement are numerable. Incorporate all of these colors within your scheme, making your favorite colors among them the most prominent.

Choose your favorite colors for flowers and landscaping. Anything goes here. Try simple evergreens with a hint of color or go all out with a multicolored planting palette. Keep the theme simple or go wild with perennial blooms.

Housebody and trim color: 1. Pittsburgh Paints—Super White 88-45

Details: 2. Pittsburgh Paints—Overcast 249-4 on shutters
   3. Pittsburgh Paints—Chickadee 113-5

For a Different Look

Try an even brighter blue on the doors and shutters, such as a deep cobalt or azure blue. This look will be more striking and bold. If blue is not your color, red is a suitable bold alternative to blue.

Taupe Beauty Gray-Brown, Taupe

I specialize in prying pearls from oysters.

—Philip Tilden, on remodeling large old houses

Brown is a classic color. It has a timeless, dependable appearance. This gray-brown almost looks like fine suede. Brown is easy to live with. It has a chameleonlike quality and seems to take on shades of the colors surrounding it. The many variations of undertone make taupe a favorite neutral to serve as a subtle background for elaborate displays of color, like those in this garden. The fantastic array of perennials and annuals and the lush trees more than compensate for potential blandness in the house color. The outcome is luxurious, subtle, and understated.

Brown need never be drab or dull, nor must it lead to a lack of visual stimulation. Simply choose the right brown, like this delicious, rich taupe, and go wild with lively landscape colors. Fancy window frames and a dash of golden yellow on doors are the main details on this Victorian.

But taupe is also suited to many other architectural styles. Imagine the clean, soft look of a fresh taupe coat on formerly tired siding. The subtlety of taupe lets the garden take center stage in this color scheme.

Housebody color: 1. Benjamin Moore—Dusty Ranch Brown
                       2105-40

Trim color: 2. Benjamin Moore—White

Details: 3. Benjamin Moore—Pearl Harbor 2165-50
                       on door panels

For a Different Look
Substitute the gold details on this house with your favorite shade of
deep blue or berry red. Both of these colors are more colorful than
the existing gold, but have a less earthy, prettier quality.

Golden Straw Beige-Brown

Things are seldom what they seem,

Skim milk masquerades as cream.

—W. S. Gilbert, *H.M.S. Pinafore*

Brown, when seen in wood tones, is so neutral that it is not often thought of as a color at all. Even people who express a dislike for brown often unconsciously surround themselves with wood floors and wood furnishings. This beige-brown, the lightest of earth tones, is soft, wholesome, and unpretentious. It has the glowing warmth of wheat fields.

A color enthusiast may think a brown house is out of the question—but look at this example. This home is beautiful without a shred of landscaping or even a wink of color. The stained wood blends in gently with the forest behind it. What a stunning effect! To achieve this look, you must start with new clapboard and stain it. White trim frames the house. If this is too neutral for your taste, the front door is the most logical place to display color.

A deep plum or crimson red on the door would give a neutral house more personality and make it stand out from the surrounding landscape. Let your door color choice be a reflection of you. Or, use a natural wooden door, such as oak, that is a darker tone than the clapboard. This will add an element of color without using paint, and maintain the rustic appeal of the house body color.

Housebody color: 1. Benjamin Moore Moorewood Siding
Stains—Desert Sand

Trim color and
details: 2. Benjamin Moore—White

For a Different Look
Treat the doors to a deep plum, midnight blue, or crimson red.
This will provide some color to the house without altering its
earthy simplicity.

Neutral Detailing

You want your home neutral and subtle but still want it noticed?
Try adding only elements of color.

Opposite, top:
Red, more than any other color, elicits strong emotions. It is interesting that red was chosen as the accent color for this neutral, charcoal colored barn. The owner must have intended his viewer to experience an emotional reaction to the barn. It sits in a tranquil environment and would probably go completely unnoticed if it weren't for its red cupola that provides strong contrast against the sky and demands your attention. For a blast of impact, add a dash of red to your home—perhaps on your front door.

Opposite, bottom:
Here is another example of a neutral house that gets its color interest from a contrasting colored natural wooden door. The wood tones have a golden-yellow glow, particularly under incandescent light at night. The brown roof shingles have strong red undertones. Both of these fixed features—the door and the roof—provide significant contrast to the neutral grays and browns of the house body. Paint color need not be used to achieve color contrast.

Above:
An old oak door is all that is needed to provide color contrast to this dark wooden and pale stucco house. Tones of red, yellow, and gold become readily apparent on the door when viewed within the context of the house. The door, while substantial in heft, actually seems to lighten the heaviness of the house merely with its lighter color. If you want contrast, you don't necessarily need to use paint color to get it. Wood has so many colorful overtones that it may be the solution for you. Natural wood is especially pleasing on doors, porches, and garage doors.

Doorways

Create enormous impact for your point of entry with colors from the Glidden Company. These identical houses are pictured with various color differences. Each façade has a distinctly different look or mood. Create the mood of your choice for your house by considering its doorway colors.

Earthy tones are used on the house, trim, and windows to make a color scheme that echoes the natural materials found in the landscape. When you combine the colors of stone and wood, the result is a low-key, easy-going welcome.

CALM

CLAPBOARD
Stone Harbor
(10YY 48/071)

TRIM
Great Smokie Mt.
(00YY 19/068)

WINDOWS
Turret Brown
(80YR 17/129)

FRESH

CLAPBOARD
Brittany Inn
(70BG 31/124)

TRIM
White Wing
(50GY 83/010)

WINDOWS
Aberdeen Place
(70RR 08/150)

Red windows, door trim, and banisters bring a real zing to the entrance of this blue house. A nice, striking contrast is created between the house color and trim colors by framing them all in white. The architectural elements of the house are accented. The colors strike a balance between cool and hot, which gives the house a lot of personality.

WARM

CLAPBOARD
Antique Linen
(30YY 70/120)

TRIM
Stowe White
(45YY 83/062)

WINDOWS
Afternoon Tea
(80YR 21/226)

The simplicity of this look is very appealing. Crisp white trim brightens the warm, pale beige house. It is inviting and cheerful.

VIBRANT

CLAPBOARD
Dover Grey
(00NN 45/000)

TRIM
Zanzibar Coast
(10YR 10/174)

WINDOWS
Deep Onyx
(00NN 07/000)

Deep, dark brown adds substance and weight to this pale gray house. Several brown paint colors were used for trim, creating interest and dimension. This house has a more majestic look than the other examples pictured here.

Hot red clapboard and a very dark brown door make this house seem heavier than most of the other examples pictured here. The house is grounded in earth colors. Beige trim keeps the contrast between the house and trim minimal. White trim would have had the opposite effect making the house seem to "jump out" at the viewer. This is a warm, earthy facade.

VIBRANT

CLAPBOARD
Old Redwood
(30YR 08/236)

TRIM
Arrow Wood
(10YY 27/060)

DOOR
Manor House
(50YR 08/038)

CALM

CLAPBOARD
Archives
(50YR 46/028)

TRIM
White Bucks
(10YY 72/021)

DOOR
Elephant
(50YR 17/029)

This very neutral paint color treatment is tranquil and calm. It has an airy, gentle quality. The clapboard is a cool beige. A taupe door adds warmth. This is a pleasant, low-key entrance.

FRESH

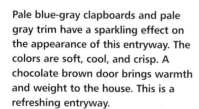

CLAPBOARD
Library Hall
(90GG 53/048)

TRIM
Grey Ghost
(50BG 83/004)

DOOR
Rowhouse
(70YR 25/106)

Pale blue-gray clapboards and pale gray trim have a sparkling effect on the appearance of this entryway. The colors are soft, cool, and crisp. A chocolate brown door brings warmth and weight to the house. This is a refreshing entryway.

WARM

CLAPBOARD
Portuguese Sonnet
(45YY 65/334)

TRIM
White on White
(30GY 88/014)

SHUTTERS
Pine Grove
(90GY 13/161)

Bright, cheery yellow clapboard makes a welcoming and friendly facade. The door is a cool green that balances the warmth of the yellow. This is an upbeat entrance.

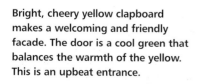

Color Schemes

The traditional approach to choosing a color scheme is to use either a complementary or an analogous scheme.

This simply means that you choose the house color, then determine paint colors for the detailing (trim, eaves, shutters, doors, and so on) in colors that have less contrast (analogous) or more contrast (complementary). Victorian and other nineteenth-century architectural styles had many features that could be highlighted with paint, and many beautifully exemplify complementary schemes. Conversely, many homes have elements that are best allowed to fade into the background. This is where an analogous color scheme is the better choice. But you can consider using paint to accentuate details or to add them where the architecture is plain or where a mood change is desired.

The color wheel displays transitions from color to color and shows their relationships. The colors on the wheel are intense and rarely used without tinting (lightening) or shading (darkening) them with black, gray, or white. The color wheel is a good tool for learning to combine colors effectively.

Analogous colors are next to or near each other on the color wheel and provide the least contrast (e.g., combining blue, blue-gray, and deep blue yields a subtle effect). An analogous scheme can literally be tints and shades of the same color, providing minimal contrast. An example of an analogous scheme is a green landscape with a pale blue house, blue-green window trim and doors, and white for the remaining trim to frame the house.

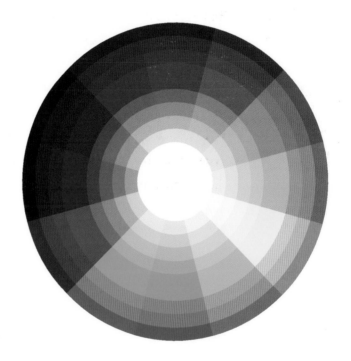

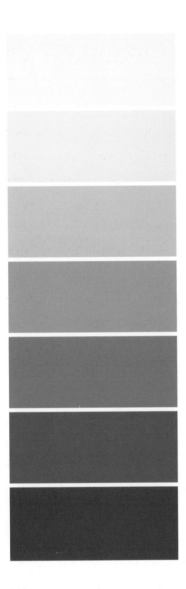

Complementary colors are directly opposite on the color wheel and provide the most dramatic contrast. A green house with a red door represents a complementary scheme. Sometimes a two-color complementary color scheme doesn't offer enough contrast to bring out the interesting details of a house. On Victorian houses, for instance, multiple colors can make the home spectacular. Or picture a Southwestern house with a terra-cotta roof. You can choose a pale tint of yellow-orange for the main house color, a darker shade or yellow-orange for the trim (eaves and fascias), and its complement, a gorgeous blue-purple, for the window trim and doors.

If you desire even more color contrast but want to ensure that the color scheme is balanced, consider these four ways to increase the complementary color palette using more than two colors. Let's take a closer look at our Southwestern house to illustrate.

1. Split complements: Yellow-orange and blue-purple are complements. Choose one for the house color. Now use the two colors adjacent to that color on the color wheel. In this case, where we chose yellow-orange for the house color, the adjacent colors are blue and purple. Consider blue for the window trim and eaves and purple

for the doors.

2. Double complements: Split two complementary colors to their adjacent colors. For example, red is the complement of green. Red-orange and red-purple are the double complements of blue-green and yellow-green.

3. Color triad: Divide colors on the wheel into a triangle. Orange, green, and purple form a triad, as do yellow, blue, and red. Selecting color triads will help to ensure a successful paint color scheme.

4. Mutual complements: Use an analogous scheme plus a complementary color. If the main color is yellow-green, then green and blue-green are the analogous colors. The complement is red, the median value of the analogous colors.

Use either an analogous or complementary scheme to determine your colors. Because you are working with paint, be sure to consider the tints and shades as you see them on the paint strip, not on the color wheel, to select the actual paint colors.

You must also consider the tints and shades—that is, the lightness and darkness of colors. To make it easier to visualize your house colors, consider creating a visual aid.

Creating a Visual Aid

Begin by taking a photograph of your house from across the street as head-on as possible. Take the shot when the house is in complete light or complete shade. Make an 8- x 10-inch (20 cm x 25 cm) print. Lay tracing paper over it. In pencil, outline the house, doors, windows, and trim. Trace outlines of trees or plantings and all fixed features. Keep the drawing simple. Once you are satisfied with your drawing, draw over the pencil lines in ink. Make three or four photocopies.

Color in the photocopies, using crayons, watercolors, or colored pencils, in several color schemes. Use ideas from other homes or magazines, books, and the color wheel. Color the grass, trees, foundation, plantings, rocks, and all other fixed features. The results may not be perfect, but they will give you a good idea of the effects of different color combinations.

American Architecture and Exterior Paint Color

Certain general house styles have been popular over time and throughout the United States. Almost all older towns and cities have examples of Colonials, Victorians, Italianate houses, bungalows, and ranches.

White is still America's favorite exterior paint color. It has been used for hundreds of years. This preference began during the Greek Revival era of 1825-1855. For years, historians mistakenly believed that ancient Greek buildings were painted in pale and muted colors. In fact, all important ancient buildings were actually painted in bright, rich greens, blues, reds, and yellows. Brilliant colors were used on buildings throughout the world.

Colonial

From the mid-1600s to about 1780, European immigrants to the New World brought along their building and color styles that would become known as Colonials. They had a limited range of pigments from which to choose. The homes usually had one or two stories and were boxlike. They were built two rooms deep and had symmetrical windows. The first Colonial homes were built mostly along the East Coast, the Gulf Coast, and in parts of the Southwest. Typical exterior colors were shades of red, orange, ocher, blue, green, gray, and brown.

Federal

From about 1780 to 1830, the Federal style dominated American architecture. Most original Federal-style homes are located on the East Coast and in portions of the South, such as Georgia and South Carolina. The Federal style is characterized by its symmetry and delicacy. Homes are usually boxlike and rectangular. They may have an elliptical fanlight over the front door and sidelights on either side of the door. There may be columns, pilasters, and curved or octagonal sections. Federal houses usually have windows recessed into arches and curving steps. Because more paint colors was available, houses were painted in a wider range of the tints and shades of existing colors, such as peach and bright green.

Greek Revival

In their first 40 years of independence, Americans gave up complex European house styles, replacing them with simple, stately homes. The Greek Revival style was first seen in Philadelphia's public buildings. Between 1825 and 1855, it became popular in the rural Northeast and the Midwest and predominated in urban houses of those regions well into the twentieth century. The form is that of a classical temple, with a front gable and portico. The front door is usually flanked by narrow sidelights and features a row of transom lights above. Wide pilasters, deep, heavy cornices, and Greek ornaments, such as the Greek fret, are characteristic. The full-colonnaded Greek mansion in Southern states became an icon in American architecture. Greek Revivals were almost always painted white.

Gothic and Italianate Revival

Between 1840 and 1900, architectural reformers offered three main new styles in place of Greek Revival designs: Gothic, Italianate, and Victorian.

Gothic

The Gothic style is characterized by the upward direction of the leading lines—vertical, steep-pitched roofs, board-and-batten siding, and sharply pointed dormers, gables, and ornamentation.

Italianate

This style was derived from the Italian villa or farmhouse and features a characteristic square tower or cupola. It has a low-pitched roof with an overhang supported by brackets. It usually has a broad veranda or porch and a flat-roofed tower. Windows are characteristically rounded.

Victorian

Victorian house styles are those popular during the reign of Britain's Queen Victoria, comprising much of the nineteenth century. With them came the concept that homes and their colors should be in harmony with nature.

Victorian houses are generally divided into two classifications: early and late. They incorporated complex shapes and ornate detailing. Characteristic of these homes are an asymmetrical facade, multicolored walls, and steeply pitched roofs, often featuring cross gables, patterned shingles, conical turrets, dormers, and decorative brackets beneath the eaves. Finials and cresting decorate roof ridges. In earlier Victorians, the mansard roof is the most distinctive feature. House color in the later Victorians included darker body colors in browns, olives, reds, and oranges. Often, these later homes had color schemes in which one color was painted on the upper body of the house and another on the lower.

Bungalow

Rustic bungalows and modest Colonials took the place of Victorians between about 1890 and 1940. By 1910, the bungalow emerged as the all-American family house. Its popularity spread from the West Coast to the East, the opposite of all previous housing fads, and the craze went on through the 1930s. The bungalow is built of natural materials such as fieldstone, cobblestone, board and batten, stucco, shingles, or clapboard. It is, ideally, a one-story structure with a wide, low-pitched roof and a front porch. The bungalow is economical, simple, and functional. Most built in the early twentieth century were painted with the same deep, rich colors as the Victorians. However, some were painted with a medium body color and white trim or a medium body color and dark trim.

Colonial Revival

The Colonial Revival became one of the dominant home styles throughout the United States during the first half of the twentieth century. Colonial Revivals were free interpretations of historical Colonials. The house has a balanced facade. Windows are symmetrically balanced with double-hung sashes. Front doors are usually surrounded with sidelights, fanlights, crown moldings, and pediments. The front entrance may be accentuated with columns or a portico. The roof may be gambrel style, center-gabled, side-gabled, or hipped. Victorian colors were replaced with primary colors, monochromatic tones, and white. Color became the enemy of form. Designers felt it detracted from the shape of the house.

Ranch House

By 1945, in postwar America, the return of 13 million service men and women created a massive housing shortage. 3,600,000 families were without homes. Ranch houses provided the solution.

Architect Cliff May created the first ranch house design in the early 1930's. He favored a Spanish Colonial style. All ranch house styles were economical to build, simple in design, informal, one-story structures, with low pitched eaves, picture windows and a rambling plan. They were enthusiastically promoted in magazines.

The ranch and its successor, the split-level, are still popular in wide ranges of color.

Note: This book does not address authentic historical color use appropriate to the date, type, and style of any building at the time of its design and construction. For this information, or for a qualified historically and scientifically trained consultant, or for information on historical preservation or restoration, call the State Historic Preservation Office, National Trust for Historic Preservation, 1785 Massachusetts Avenue, Washington, D.C. 20036, or a regional office of the National Park Service.

Photo Credits

Sandy Agrafiotis, 11 (top); 68

Courtesy of The Glidden Company, 28; 120; 121

Sam Gray, 11 (second from bottom); 13 (top & middle); 32; 33; 51; 58; 61; 109; 126; 127; 132

Peter Gridley/FPG International, 56

James R. Salomon, 40; 96; 110; 129

The Society for the Preservation of New England Antiquities, 49; 103

Douglas Keister, 11 (bottom); 12 (second from top); 39; 44; 45; 46; 54; 55; 66; 70; 71; 77; 81; 93; 99; 100; 104; 105; 115; 118; 119; 130; 131; 133

Eric Roth, 1 (right); 12 (middle); 13 (bottom); 72; 84; 89; 90; 119 (top)

Brian Vanden Brink, 1 (left & middle); 12 (top, second from bottom & bottom); 30; 37; 43; 63; 65; 75; 79; 86; 107; 113; 128

Brian Vanden Brink/Quinn Evans, Architect, 82

Brian Vanden Brink/James Sterling, Architect, 83

Brian Vanden Brink/Rick Burt, Architect, 94

Brian Vanden Brink/Mark Hutker Architects, 95

Brian Vanden Brink/Warren Hall, Architect, 117

David Wakely/Cathy Schwabe/EHDD Architecture, ©2001, 53

Dedication

To Penny and Elise

Acknowledgments

This book has taken several years to write and photograph; many more years were spent on-site at paint color consultations accumulating knowledge. My gratitude goes to everyone who worked on the book. My agent, Amye Dyer, for her continual support and friendship. My appreciation goes to Shawna Mullen, my editor, whose belief in the project and gentleness of spirit helped along the way; to Betsy Gammons, my photo editor, whose expertise made it possible to acquire so many superb photographs; to all of the photographers for the beautiful images, especially Sam Gray for trekking his equipment out in the snow. To Ann Fox for editing and organizing all the final materials; and most of all to my sister Penny for her support and enormous input.

About the Author

Bonnie Rosser Krims is the author of *The Perfect Palette* (Warner Books) and one of a handful of nationally recognized professional paint-color consultants in the United States. She is also an accomplished painter whose work has been widely exhibited.

Bonnie's consulting business is based in Massachusetts, but she consults with clients throughout the country. You can contact her at BKrims@aol.com, through her Web site, theperfectpalette.com, or at the Emerson Umbrella Center for the Arts, 40 Stow Street, Concord, Massachusetts 01742, telephone (978) 371-9204.